THE ULTIMATE NINJA FOODI DIGITAL AIR FRYER OVEN COOKBOOK.

1900 Days Affordable, Easy and Delicious Recipes for Beginners to Bake, Air Fry, Broil, Grill, Roast, Dehydrate. Anyone can cook.

Jennifer Nelson

TABLE OF CONTENTS

Meat Recipes 37

Fish and Seafood Recipes 47

Vegetables and Sides Dishes 57

Snacks and Appetizer Recipes 66

Dessert Recipes 74

Introduction

The Ninja Digital Air Fry Oven is the ultimate kitchen companion, thanks to several advanced features. Unlike traditional ovens or air fryers, the Ninja Foodi Air Fry oven has an adjustable space feature, allowing you to position the oven both horizontally and vertically on a kitchen shelf. The oven can be used in a horizontal position for cooking. When not in use, the cleaned oven can be flipped vertically to stand on the shelf. This adds a little extra space above the shelf without doing much. Just make sure the oven is completely cool and clean before flipping it.

This Air Fry oven has eight functions all in one. With the press of a button, a user can Air fry, Air roast, bake, toast bread and bagels, dehydrate, and broil food. You can also switch between modes while cooking if necessary. The toast and bagel functions allow you to customise the darkness of the bread. If you're unsure how to use all of its advanced cooking features, try all of the recipes in this cookbook! Here are a few tasty ideas for making the most of your Air fryer oven.

Ninja Foodi Digital Air Fry Oven is well known for its energy-saving technology. The device consumes 1800 watts per hour and heats up quickly to the desired temperature. Air fry and bake your favourite meal in a matter of seconds. The device also keeps the food warm until it is ready to be served. One of the best features of the Ninja Air Fry oven is that it also functions as a toaster.

This oven has two toasting options: bread and bagels. To toast the bread, press the Toast button, and to toast the bagel, press the Bagel mode. The bars of darkness represent the degree of darkness desired for the toast. You can have everything from lightly soft brown toast to dark brown crispy toast this way.

The control panel on the Ninja Foodi Air Fryer oven is extremely user-friendly. It has a different button for each function as well as a dial to switch between modes and adjust the time and temperature.

The Ninja Foodi Digital Air Fry Oven is the best kitchen appliance if you want to feed your family healthy and delicious food in less time.

Benefits of Using Ninja Foodi Air Fryer Oven

1. Time Saving.
With only 24 hours to complete everyday routine tasks, the time has become a genuinely luxury in our fast-paced lifestyle. Air Fryers are designed to save your precious cooking time by serving you crunchy snacks and fried cuisines in a matter of-minutes. If you are always on a tight schedule, Air Fryer is no less than a time savior.

2. Protect the Food's Nutrients.
Unlike deep frying, Air Fryers do not deconstruct the food's good nutrients and add on bad fats. If you think your yasai tempura (deep fried battered vegetables) are healthy, here is news for you; while they may look like they are full of nutritious elements, the deep-frying process would have destroyed the beneficial vitamins and minerals contained in the vegetables.

3. Superfast Heating.
Unlike traditional frying method, Air Fryers takes only a few-minutes to heat and prepare foods. They are always ready to make meals whenever you crave for fried foods

Most Air Fryer models get ready in only 3-minutes to heat up properly and they can also go as high as 400 Degrees °F or (204 Degrees °C) to make you crispy meals.

4. Calories Are Good, But Too Much Spells Trouble.
Fried foods are high in calories which is the leading cause of weight gain and obesity. Obesity will then lead to a plethora of killer diseases such as diabetes, cancer, stroke, sleep problems and immobility to name a few.

Adopting a low-fat diet will help you maintain your weight or prevent weight loss because essentially, you are eating fewer calories. Therefore, eating Air Fryer-cooked food will support your weight loss journey.

5. Build A Fortress for Your Heart.
Eating food fried with an Air Fryer reduces the risk of heart diseases and protects your body by helping you absorb necessary nutrients. Since minimal amount of oil is used to prepare food, you can be sure that your body will not accumulate excessive fats in the long run. Instead, the optimal amount of oil used will help your body protect your heart.

6. Fat Is Not All Bad.

Fat is a macronutrient – it is essential to help control inflammation, blood clotting, maintaining healthy hair and skin, prevent heart diseases, provide energy and assist in the absorption of vitamins A, D, E and K. While it is important to your bodily functions, too much of it is detrimental to health.

An Air Fryer is a modern kitchen appliance that fries food using heated hot air by using at most a tbsp. of oil. This way, you are able to eat fried food without worrying about the negative effects of fatty food on your health.

7. Reduces risk of certain diseases.

Cooking food in an air fryer can help you avoid trans-fat which are considered harmful processed fats that raise the risk for type 2 diabetes and heart related diseases.

The majority of restaurants deep-fry food in trans-fat containing vegetable oils such as canola and research has shown that reusing oil can raise cholesterol and blood pressure leading to vascular inflammation. Replacing deep-frying with air frying can reduce your risk of these complications.

Functions and Buttons

AIR FRY: Make foods that would traditionally be fried—such as chicken wings, French fries, and chicken nuggets— with little to no added oil.

AIR ROAST: Achieve a crispy outside and perfectly cooked inside for full-sized sheet pan meals, thicker proteins, and roasted veggies.

AIR BROIL: Broils meat and fish and evenly browns the tops of casseroles.

BAKE: Evenly bakes everything from your favorite cookies to homemade pizzas.

TOAST: Evenly toasts up to 9 slices of bread to your perfect level of darkness.

BAGEL: Perfectly toast up to 9 slices of bagels halves when they're placed cut-side up on the wire rack.

DEHYDRATE: Dehydrates meats, fruits, and vegetables for healthy snacks.

KEEP WARM: Keeps food warm up to 2 hours.

CONTROL PANEL DISPLAY & OPERATING BUTTONS

1 Time display: Shows the cook time. The time will count down when cooking is in progress.

2 Temperature display: Shows the cook temperature. Time and temperature will always return to the cook time and temperature that was set the last time the oven was in use.

3 PRE: flashes when the unit is preheating.

4 "FLIP" will appear on the time display when the unit is cool enough to flip up for storage or cleaning.

6 SLICE and **DARK** will illuminate when using the Toast or Bagel function.

7 START/PAUSE button: Press to start or pause cooking.

8 Function/Time/Temperature dial: Turn to select a cooking function or adjust time and temperature (or number of slices and darkness level when using the Toast and Bagel functions). Press and hold the START/PAUSE button for 3 Seconds to return to the function selection.

9 TIME/SLICE button: To select a cook time. press the TIME button. then use the dial to adjust the time. When using the Toast or Bagel function. this button will adjust the number of slices instead of the time.

10 TEMP/DARKNESS button: To adjust temperature. press the TEMP button and use the dial to adjust the temperature.

When using the Toast or Bagel function. this button will adjust the darkness level instead of the temperature. The cook time and temperature may be adjusted at any time during the cooking cycle. To switch from Fahrenheit to Celsius. press and hold the TEMP/DARKNESS button for 3 seconds while the unit is not in cook mode.

11 (Light) button: Press to turn the over's interior light on and off. The light will automatically turn on when there are 30 seconds of cook time remaining.

12 (Power) button: Press to turn the unit on and off.

Using Your Foodi Digital Air Fry Oven

The Ninja Foodi Digital Air Fry Oven's primary function is Air Fry. It can also perform a variety of cooking functions, including air broil, air roast, bake, toast, dehydrate, keep warm, and bagel. The digital display helps in keeping track of the temperature and cooking time settings. When in bagel or toast mode, the display also shows the slice and darkness settings.

USING THE COOKING FUNCTIONS

To turn on the unit, plug the power cord into the wall, flip oven down into cooking position, and press the Power button.

Air Fry:

One of the healthiest cooking techniques is air frying because it uses less oil or fat to cook the meal. When using the air fry cooking mode, only 1 tablespoon of oil is required to make French fries, crispy beans, chicken wings, and chicken nuggets. You get food that is juicy, crispy, and tender. Use the air fry cooking feature to recreate your favourite fried meal.

1. To select the function, turn the dial until AIR FRY illuminates. The default time and temperature settings will display.

2. Press the TIME/SLICE button and use the dial to select your time up to 1 hour. To set the time, press the TIME/SLICE button again.

3. Then press the TEMP/DARKNESS button and use the dial to select a temperature between 250°F–450°F. To set the temperature, press the TEMP/DARKNESS button again.

4. Press START/PAUSE to begin preheating.

5. Place ingredients in the air fry basket. If ingredients are fatty, oily, or marinated, place the basket on the sheet pan. Use air fry basket for dry ingredients. Use air fry basket with sheet pan underneath for fatty, oily, or marinated ingredients.

6. When the unit beeps to signify it has preheated, immediately slide the basket into the upper rails of the oven. If also using the sheet pan, slide both into the oven at the same time, with the basket in the upper rails and the pan on the wire rack beneath the basket. Close oven door.

NOTE: The timer will start counting down as soon as the unit has preheated. If ingredients are not ready to go into the oven, simply turn the dial to add more time.

7. For more even browning and crispiness, toss ingredients or turn the basket 180° halfway through cooking cycle.

8. When cook time is complete, the unit will beep.

Air Roast:

The Ninja Foodi Digital Air Fry Oven can cook all sheet pan meals, including sheet pan fajitas. It produces food with a tender and light brown texture. You can roast your favourite foods such as vegetables, beef, chicken, seafood, and lamb using the air roast cooking function. Without a doubt, the Ninja Foodi Digital Air Fry Oven is an expert at air roasting.

1. To select the function, turn the dial until AIR ROAST illuminates. The default time and temperature settings will display.

2. Press the TIME/SLICE button and use the dial to select your time up to 2 hours. To set the time, press TIME/SLICE button again.

NOTE: If cooking for 1 hour or less, the clock will count down by minutes and seconds. If cooking for more than 1 hour, the clock will count down by hours and minutes.

3. Press the TEMP/DARKNESS button and use the dial to select a temperature between 250°F–450°F. To set the temperature, press the TEMP/DARKNESS button again.

4. Press START/PAUSE to begin preheating.

NOTE: Food cooks faster when using the Air Roast function than when using the Bake function, so for traditional oven recipes, lower the cook time 30% and lower the temperature 25°F.

5. Place ingredients on the sheet pan. When the unit beeps to signify it has preheated, immediately place the sheet pan on the wire rack. Close oven door.

NOTE: The timer will start counting down as soon as the unit has preheated. If ingredients are not ready to go into the oven, simply turn the dial to add more time.

6. During cooking, you can open the oven door to check on or flip ingredients.

7. When cook time is complete, the unit will beep.

Air Broil:

Cooking time is reduced when using the air broil cooking mode. With the air broil function, you can get crispy and perfect texture food in about twenty minutes on average. You can broil your favourite foods such as chicken, vegetables, fruits, and seafood, among others.

1. To select the function, turn the dial until AIR BROIL illuminates. The default time and temperature settings will display.

2. Press the TIME/SLICE button and use the dial to select your time up to 30 minutes. To set the time, press the TIME/SLICE button again.

3. Press the TEMP/DARKNESS button and use the dial to select either HI or LO. To set the temperature, press the TEMP/DARKNESS button again.

4. Place ingredients on the sheet pan. Place the sheet pan on the wire rack and close the oven door, press START/STOP to start cooking.

5. During cooking, you can open the oven door to check on or flip ingredients.

6. When cook time is complete, the unit will beep

Bake:

You can also bake muffins, pizza, bread, cakes, cupcakes, brownies, and vegetables in bake mode. Everyone's favourite cooking function is baking. This option is appropriate for special occasions.

1. To select the function, turn the dial until BAKE illuminates. The default time and temperature settings will display.

2. Press the TIME/SLICE button and use the dial to select your time up to 2 hours. To set the time, press the TIME/SLICE button again.

NOTE: If cooking for 1 hour or less, the clock will count down by minutes and seconds. If cooking for more than 1 hour, the clock will count down by hours and minutes.

3. Press the TEMP/DARKNESS button and use the dial to select a temperature between 250°F–450°F. To set the temperature, press the TEMP/DARKNESS button again.

4. Press START/PAUSE to begin preheating.

5. Place ingredients on the sheet pan. When the unit beeps to signify it has preheated, immediately place the sheet pan on the wire rack. Close oven door.

NOTE: The timer will start counting down as soon as the unit has preheated. If ingredients are not ready to go into the oven, simply turn the dial to add more time.

6. During cooking, you can open the oven door to check on or flip ingredients.

7. When cook time is complete, the unit will beep.

Toast:

The Ninja Foodi Digital Air Fry Oven can toast nine slices of bread at once. On the control panel, you can adjust the bread's darkness. You no longer need a separate appliance to toast the bread.

1. To select the function, turn the dial until TOAST illuminates. The default amount of slices and darkness will be displayed.

2. Press the TIME/SLICE button and use the dial to select the number of bread slices. You may toast up to 9 slices at once. To set the number of slices, press the TIME/SLICE button again.

3. Press the TEMP/DARKNESS button and use the dial to select a darkness level. To set the darkness level, press the TEMP/DARKNESS button again.

NOTE: There is no temperature adjustment available for the Toast function, and the unit does not preheat in Toast mode. It is very important to select the exact number of slices to avoid over- or under-toasting.

4. Place bread slices on the wire rack. Close oven door and press START/PAUSE to begin cooking.

5. You do not need to flip the slices during cooking. When cook time is complete, the unit will beep.

Bagel:

This function is similar to the toast function. You can now use this function to prepare bagel halves. Using the Ninja Foodi Digital Air Fry oven, you will get crispy, golden, and delicious bagels. The display indicates whether you want to darken or lighten the bagel.

1. To select the function, turn the dial until BAGEL illuminates. The default number of slices and darkness level will display.

2. Press the TIME/SLICE button and use the dial to select the number of slices. You may toast up to 9 bagel slices at once. To set the number of slices, press the TIME/SLICE button again.

3. Press the TEMP/DARKNESS button and use the dial to select a darkness level. To set the darkness level, press the TEMP/DARKNESS button again.

NOTE: There is no temperature adjustment available for the Bagel function, and the unit does not preheat in Bagel mode. It is very important to select the exact number of slices to avoid over- or under-toasting.

4. Place bagel slices, cut-side up, on the wire rack. Close oven door and press START/PAUSE to begin cooking.

5. You do not need to flip the slices during cooking. When cook time is complete, the unit will beep.

Dehydrate:

Fruit, jerky, dried fruit, vegetables, and other foods can be dehydrated. This cooking function typically takes 10 to 11 hours to complete. It provides you with perfect, delectable, and healthy food. The longer you wait, the more dehydrated your food will become.

NOTE: The DEHYDRATE function is not included on all models.

1. To select the function, turn the dial until DEHYDRATE illuminates. The default time and temperature settings will display.

2. Press the TIME/SLICE button and use the dial to select a time up to 12 hours. To set the time, press the TIME/SLICE button again.

3. Press the TEMP/DARKNESS button and use the dial to select a temperature between 105°F–195°F. To set the temperature, press the TEMP/DARKNESS button again.

4. Place ingredients in the air fry basket and place basket in oven. Close oven door and press START/PAUSE to begin cooking.

5. During cooking, you can open the oven door to check on or flip ingredients.

6. When cook time is complete, the unit will beep.

Keep Warm:

You can keep your food warm for up to 2 hours using this function. You no longer need to reheat the food. If you have time to serve the food, you can keep it warm by using this cooking mode. With the Ninja Foodi Digital Air Fry Oven function, the food is perfectly preserved and perfectly warm.

NOTE: The Keep Warm function is not included on all models.

1. To select the function, turn the dial until KEEP WARM illuminates. The default time setting will display.

2. Press the TIME/SLICE button and use the dial to select a time up to 2 hours. To set the time, press the TIME/SLICE button again.

NOTE: There is no temperature selection available for the Keep Warm function.

3. Place food on the sheet pan or in an oven-safe container and place the pan or container on the wire rack. Close oven door and press START/PAUSE to begin warming.

NOTE: The unit does not preheat in Keep Warm mode.

4. When warming time is complete, the unit will beep.

Cleaning, Maintenance & Storage

EVERYDAY CLEANING:

The unit should be cleaned thoroughly after every use.

1. Unplug the unit from the outlet and allow it to cool down before cleaning.

2. Empty crumb tray by sliding it out of the oven when the oven is in the flipped-down position.

NOTE: Empty crumb tray frequently. Hand-wash when necessary.

3. To clean any food splatter on the interior walls of the unit, wipe them with a soft, damp sponge.

4. To clean the exterior of the main unit and the control panel, wipe them clean with a damp cloth. A non-abrasive liquid cleanser or mild spray solution may be used. Apply the cleanser to the sponge, not the oven surface, before cleaning.

DEEP CLEANING:

1. Unplug the unit from the outlet and allow it to cool down before cleaning.

2. Remove all accessories from the unit, including the crumb tray, and wash separately. Use a non-abrasive cleaning brush to more thoroughly wash the air fry basket.

3. Flip up the oven into the storage position.

4. Press the push button to release the back door to access the oven's interior.

5. Use warm, soapy water and a soft cloth to wash the oven's interior. DO NOT use abrasive cleaners, scrubbing brushes, or chemical cleaners, as they will damage the oven.

CAUTION: NEVER put the main unit in the dishwasher or immerse it in water or any other liquid.

NOTE: Deep cleaning instructions continued on next page.

6. Only the sheet pan and air fry basket are dishwasher safe.

7. Thoroughly dry all parts before placing them back in the oven.

FLIP-UP-AND-AWAY STORAGE:

1. DO NOT flip oven up when is illuminated. Wait for oven to cool down before handling. Hold handles on each side of the unit.

2. Lift and flip unit upward.

3. Leave the unit in the upright position when storing or for deep cleaning.

Breakfast Recipes

Potato and Corned Beef Casserole

Ingredients for Serving: 3

2 garlic cloves, minced.	3 eggs
3 Yukon Gold potatoes	2 tbsp. unsalted butter.
½ of onion, chopped.	2 tbsp. vegetable oil
12 oz. corned beef	½ tsp. salt

Directions and Ready in About: 1 hr. 35-Minutes.

- Press *Power* button of "Ninja Foodi Digital Air Fry Oven" and turn the dial to select *Bake* mode. Press *Time/Slice* button and again turn the dial to set the cooking time to 30 minutes.
- Now, push *Temp/Darkness* button and rotate the dial to set the temperature at 350 Degrees °F or (176 Degrees °C). Press *Start/Pause* button to start your Air Fry Oven.
- When the unit beeps to show that it is preheated, open the oven door and grease the air fry basket.
- Place the potatoes into the prepared air fry basket and insert in the oven. When cooking time is completed, open the oven door and transfer the potatoes onto a tray.
- Set aside to cool for about 15 minutes. After cooling, cut the potatoes into ½-inch-thick slices.
- In a skillet, melt the butter over medium heat and cook the onion and garlic for about 10 minutes. Remove from the heat and place the onion mixture into a casserole dish.
- Add the potato slices, oil, salt and corned beef and mix well. Press *Power* button of "Ninja Foodi Digital Air Fry Oven" and turn the dial to select *Bake* mode.
- Press *Time/Slice* button and again turn the dial to set the cooking time to 40 minutes. Now, push *Temp/Darkness* button and rotate the dial to set the temperature at 350 Degrees °F or (176 Degrees °C).
- Press *Start/Pause* button to start your Air Fry Oven. When the unit beeps to show that it is preheated, open the oven door.
- Arrange the casserole dish over the wire rack and insert in the oven. After 30 minutes of cooking, remove the casserole dish and crack 3 eggs on top.

- When cooking time is completed, open the oven door and serve immediately with fresh baby kale.

Nutrition Values Per Serving: Calories: 542; Fat: 35.6g; Sat Fat: 14.1g; Carbs: 33.1g; Fiber: 2.8g; Sugar: 2.3g; Protein: 24.7g

Pumpkin Muffins

Ingredients for Serving: 6

2 medium eggs, beaten.	1 cup pumpkin puree.
½ cup honey	2 cups oats
1 tbsp. vanilla essence.	
1 tbsp. cocoa nibs	1 tsp. nutmeg
1 tsp. coconut butter.	

Directions and Ready in About: 30-Minutes.

- Whisk all ingredients in a mixer until smooth. Divide this pumpkin oat batter into a 12-cup muffin tray. Transfer the tray to the "Ninja Foodi Digital Air Fry Oven" and close the door.
- Select *Air Fry* mode by rotating the dial. Press the *Time/Slice* button and change the value to 15 minutes.
- Press the *Temp/Darkness* button and change the value to 360 Degrees °F or (182 Degrees °C). Press *Start/Pause* to begin cooking. Serve fresh with morning pudding.

Nutrition Values Per Serving: Calories: 234; Fat: 5.1g; Sodium: 231mg; Carbs: 46g; Fiber: 5g; Sugar: 2.1g; Protein: 7g

Cheesy Eggs in Avocado Cups

Ingredients for Serving: 2

1 large ripe avocado, halved and pitted

2 tbsp. Parmesan cheese, grated.

2 eggs

1 tsp. fresh chives, minced.

Pinch of cayenne pepper

Salt and ground black pepper, to taste.

Directions and Ready in About: 32-Minutes.

- With a spoon, scoop out some of the flesh from the avocado halves to make a hole. Arrange the avocado halves onto a baking pan.
- Crack 1 egg into each avocado half and sprinkle with salt and black pepper. Press *Power* button of "Ninja Foodi Digital Air Fry Oven" and turn the dial to select *Air Fry* mode.
- Press *Time/Slice* button and again turn the dial to set the cooking time to 22 minutes. Now, push *Temp/Darkness* button and rotate the dial to set the temperature at 350 Degrees °F or (176 Degrees °C).
- Press *Start/Pause* button to start your Air Fry Oven. When the unit beeps to show that it is preheated, open the oven door and grease the air fry basket.
- Arrange the avocado halves into the air fry basket and insert in the oven. After 12 minutes of cooking, sprinkle the top of avocado halves with Parmesan cheese.
- When cooking time is completed, open the oven door and transfer the avocado halves onto a platter. Sprinkle with cayenne pepper and serve hot with the garnishing of chives alongside baby greens.

Nutrition Values Per Serving: Calories: 286; Fat: 25.2g; Sat Fat: 6.1g; Carbs: 9g; Fiber: 0.9g; Sugar: 0.9g; Protein: 9.5g

Cheesy Cream Omelet

Ingredients for Serving: 2

¼ cup cream

¼ cup Cheddar cheese, grated.

4 eggs

1 tsp. fresh parsley, minced.

Salt and ground black pepper, to taste.

Directions and Ready in About: 18-Minutes.

- Take a bowl, add the eggs, cream, parsley, salt and black pepper and beat well. Place the egg mixture into a small baking pan.

- Press *Power* button of "Ninja Foodi Digital Air Fry Oven" and turn the dial to select *Air Fry* mode. Press *Time/Slice* button and again turn the dial to set the cooking time to 8 minutes.
- Now, push *Temp/Darkness* button and rotate the dial to set the temperature at 350 Degrees °F or (176 Degrees °C).
- Press *Start/Pause* button to start your Air Fry Oven. When the unit beeps to show that it is preheated, open the oven door.
- Arrange a sheet pan over the wire rack and insert in the oven. After 4 minutes, sprinkle the omelet with cheese evenly.
- When cooking time is completed, open the oven door and remove the sheet pan. Cut the omelet into 2 portions and serve hot alongside the toasted bread slices.

Nutrition Values Per Serving: Calories: 202; Fat: 15.1g; Sat Fat: 6.8g; Carbs: 1.8g; Fiber: 0g; Sugar: 1.4g; Protein: 14.8g

Walnut and Banana Bread

Ingredients for Serving: 10

1½ cups self-rising flour.

¼ tsp. bicarbonate of soda

5 tbsp. plus 1 tsp. butter.

⅔ cup plus ½ tbsp. caster sugar

2 medium eggs

3½ oz. walnuts, chopped.

2 cups bananas, peeled and mashed.

Directions and Ready in About: 40-Minutes.

- Take a bowl, mix the flour and bicarbonate of soda together. In another bowl, add the butter and sugar and beat until pale and fluffy.
- Add the eggs, one at a time, along with a little flour and mix well. Stir in the remaining flour and walnuts. Add the bananas and mix until well combined.
- Grease a loaf pan. Place the mixture into the prepared pan. Press *Power* button of "Ninja Foodi Digital Air Fry Oven" and turn the dial to select the *Air Fry* mode.
- Press *Time/Slice* button and again turn the dial to set the cooking time to 10 minutes. Now, push *Temp/Darkness* button and rotate the dial to set the temperature at 355 Degrees °F or (179 Degrees °C).

- Press *Start/Pause* button to start your Air Fry Oven. When the unit beeps to show that it is preheated, open the oven door.
- Arrange the pan into the air fry basket and insert in the oven. After 10 minutes of cooking, set the temperature at 340 Degrees °F or (171 Degrees °C) for 15 minutes.
- When cooking time is completed, open the oven door and place the pan onto a wire rack to cool for about 10 minutes.
- Carefully invert the bread onto the wire rack to cool completely before slicing. Cut the bread into desired sized slices and serve with strawberry jam.

Nutrition Values Per Serving: Calories: 270; Fat: 12.8g; Sat Fat: 4.3g; Carbs: 35.5g; Fiber: 2g; Sugar: 17.2g; Protein: 5.8g

Zucchini Fritters

Ingredients for Serving: 4

7 oz. Halloumi cheese	¼ cup all-purpose flour
2 eggs	1 tsp. fresh dill, minced.
10½ oz. zucchini, grated and squeezed.	Salt and ground black pepper, to taste.

Directions and Ready in About: 22-Minutes.

- Take a large bowl and mix all the ingredients together. Make small-sized fritters from the mixture. Press *Power* button of "Ninja Foodi Digital Air Fry Oven" and turn the dial to select *Air Fry* mode.
- Press *Time/Slice* button and again turn the dial to set the cooking time to 7 minutes. Now, push *Temp/Darkness* button and rotate the dial to set the temperature at 355 Degrees °F or (179 Degrees °C).
- Press *Start/Pause* button to start your Air Fry Oven. When the unit beeps to show that it is preheated, open the oven door.
- Arrange fritters into the greased sheet pan and insert in the oven. When cooking time is completed, open the oven door and serve warm with the topping of sour cream.

Nutrition Values Per Serving: Calories: 253; Fat: 17.2g; Sat Fat: 1.4g; Carbs: 10g; Fiber: 1.1g; Sugar: 2.7g; Protein: 15.2g

Bacon, Spinach and Egg Cups

Ingredients for Serving: 3

6 cooked bacon slices, chopped.	3 tbsp. Parmesan cheese, grated.
⅓ cup heavy cream	Salt and ground black pepper, to taste.
2 cups fresh baby spinach	
3 eggs	

Directions and Ready in About: 31-Minutes.

- Heat a nonstick skillet over medium-high heat and cook the bacon for about 5 minutes. Add the spinach and cook for about 2-3 minutes.
- Stir in the heavy cream and Parmesan cheese and cook for about 2-3 minutes. Remove from the heat and set aside to cool slightly.
- Grease 3 (3-inch) ramekins. Crack 1 egg in each prepared ramekin and top with bacon mixture. Press *Power* button of "Ninja Foodi Digital Air Fry Oven" and turn the dial to select *Air Fry* mode.
- Press *Time/Slice* button and again turn the dial to set the cooking time to 5 minutes. Now, push *Temp/Darkness* button and rotate the dial to set the temperature at 350 Degrees °F or (176 Degrees °C).
- Press *Start/Pause* button to start your Air Fry Oven. When the unit beeps to show that it is preheated, open the oven door and grease the air fry basket.
- Arrange the ramekins into the air fry basket and insert in the oven. When cooking time is completed, open the oven door and sprinkle each ramekin with salt and black pepper. Serve hot alongside the English muffins.

Nutrition Values Per Serving: Calories: 442; Fat: 34.5g; Sat Fat: 12.9g; Carbs: 2.3g; Fiber: 0.5g; Sugar: 0.4g; Protein: 29.6g

Breakfast Sausage Bake

Ingredients for Serving: 6

24 oz. bulk pork sausage.	2 cups shredded Cheddar cheese
3 cups frozen hash brown potatoes	1 cup Bisquick mix.
1 medium bell pepper, chopped.	2 cups milk
	4 eggs

1 medium onion, chopped.   ¼ tsp. pepper.

Directions and Ready in About: 1 hr. 5-Minutes.

- Whisk Bisquick with milk, eggs and pepper in a mixer. Sauté pork sausage, onion and bell pepper in a 10-inch skillet over medium heat.
- Stir cook until the sausage turns brown in color, then transfer to a casserole dish. Toss in potatoes, 1 ½ cups of cheese and the Bisquick mixture.
- Transfer the casserole dish to the "Ninja Foodi Digital Air Fry Oven" and close the door. Select *Bake* mode by rotating the dial.
- Press the *Time/Slice* button and change the value to 45 minutes. Press the *Temp/Darkness* button and change the value to 350 Degrees °F or (176 Degrees °C).
- Press *Start/Pause* to begin cooking. Drizzle the remaining cheese over the casserole and bake for 5 minutes. Serve with crispy bacon and bread.

Nutrition Values Per Serving: Calories: 297; Fat: 15g; Sodium: 202mg; Carbs: 58.5g; Fiber: 4g; Sugar: 1g; Protein: 33g

Spinach and Pancetta Frittata

Ingredients for Serving: 2

¼ cup fresh baby spinach

¼ cup Parmesan cheese, grated.

¼ cup pancetta

½ of tomato, cubed.

3 eggs

Salt and ground black pepper, to taste.

Directions and Ready in About: 31-Minutes.

- Heat a nonstick skillet over medium heat and cook the pancetta for about 5 minutes. Add the tomato and spinach cook for about 2-3 minutes.
- Remove from the heat and drain the grease from skillet. Set aside to cool slightly. Meanwhile, in a small bowl, add the eggs, salt and black pepper and beat well.
- In the bottom of a greased sheet pan, place the pancetta mixture and top with the eggs, followed by the cheese.
- Press *Power* button of "Ninja Foodi Digital Air Fry Oven" and turn the dial to select *Air Fry* mode.
- Press *Time/Slice* button and again turn the dial to set the cooking time to 8 minutes. Now, push *Temp/Darkness* button and rotate the dial to set the temperature at 355 Degrees °F or (179 Degrees °C).
- Press *Start/Pause* button to start your Air Fry Oven. When the unit beeps to show that it is preheated, open the oven door.
- Arrange the pan over the wire rack and insert in the oven. When cooking time is completed, open the oven door and remove the baking dish. Cut into equal-sized wedges and serve alongside the green salad.

Nutrition Values Per Serving: Calories: 287; Fat: 20.8g; Sat Fat: 7.2g; Carbs: 1.7g; Fiber: 0.3g; Sugar: 0.9g; Protein: 23.1g

Cheese and Ham Scones

Ingredients for Serving: 6

2 cups all-purpose flour

4 oz. cheddar cheese, shredded.

¼ cup milk

¾ cup heavy cream

¼ cup scallion, chopped.

1 cup ham, diced, cooked.

1 tbsp. baking powder

2 tbsp. butter, cubed.

2 tsp. sugar

1 tsp. kosher salt.

Directions and Ready in About: 40-Minutes.

- Whisk baking powder with flour, sugar, salt and butter in a mixing bowl. Beat milk, cream, ham, scallion and cheddar cheese in another bowl.
- Stir in the flour-butter mixture and mix well until it forms a smooth dough. Place this scones dough on a floured surface and spread it into a 7-inch round sheet.
- Cut this dough sheet into 6 wedges of equal size. Place these wedges in the cooking pan, lined with parchment paper.
- Transfer the pan to the "Ninja Foodi Digital Air Fry Oven" and close the door. Select *Bake* mode by rotating the dial.
- Press the *Time/Slice* button and change the value to 25 minutes. Press the *Temp/Darkness* button and change the value to 400 Degrees °F or (204 Degrees °C).
- Press *Start/Pause* to begin cooking. When baked, serve the scones with morning eggs with the cream cheese dip.

Nutrition Values Per Serving: Calories: 387; Fat: 6g; Sodium: 154mg; Carbs: 37.4g; Fiber: 2.9g; Sugar: 15g; Protein: 15g

Savory Parsley Soufflé

Ingredients for Serving: 2

2 eggs

2 tbsp. light cream

1 fresh red chili pepper, chopped.

1 tbsp. fresh parsley, chopped.

Salt, to taste.

Directions and Ready in About: 18-Minutes.

- Grease 2 soufflé dishes. Take a bowl, add all the ingredients and beat until well combined. Divide the mixture into prepared soufflé dishes.
- Press *Power* button of "Ninja Foodi Digital Air Fry Oven" and turn the dial to select *Air Fry* mode.
- Press *Time/Slice* button and again turn the dial to set the cooking time to 8 minutes. Now, push *Temp/Darkness* button and rotate the dial to set the temperature at 390 Degrees °F or (199 Degrees °C).
- Press *Start/Pause* button to start your Air Fry Oven. When the unit beeps to show that it is preheated, open the oven door and grease the air fry basket.
- Arrange the soufflé dishes into the air fry basket and insert in the oven. When cooking time is completed, open the oven door and serve hot alongside a piece of crusty bread.

Nutrition Values Per Serving: Calories: 108; Fat: 9g; Sat Fat: 4.3g; Carbs: 1.1g; Fiber: 0.22g; Sugar: 0.5g; Protein: 6g

Sweet Potato Rosti

Ingredients for Serving: 2

½ lb. sweet potatoes, peeled, grated and squeezed

Salt and ground black pepper, to taste.

1 tbsp. fresh parsley, chopped finely.

Directions and Ready in About: 30-Minutes.

- Take a large bowl, mix the grated sweet potato, parsley, salt and black pepper together. Arrange the sweet potato mixture into the lightly greased sheet pan and shape it into an even circle.
- Press *Power* button of "Ninja Foodi Digital Air Fry Oven" and turn the dial to select *Air Fry* mode. Press *Time/Slice* button and again turn the dial to set the cooking time to 15 minutes.
- Now, push *Temp/Darkness* button and rotate the dial to set the temperature at 355 Degrees °F or (179 Degrees °C).
- Press *Start/Pause* button to start your Air Fry Oven. When the unit beeps to show that it is preheated, open the oven door and insert the sheet pan in oven.
- When cooking time is completed, open the oven door Cut the sweet potato rosti into wedges and serve immediately alongside the yogurt dip.

Nutrition Values Per Serving: Calories: 160; Fat: 2.1g; Sat Fat: 1.4g; Carbs: 30.3g; Fiber: 4.7g; Sugar: 0.6g; Protein: 2.2g

Blueberry Scones

Ingredients for Serving: 6

8 oz. coconut milk

1 cup fresh blueberries

¼ oz. lemon zest.

1 tbsp. baking powder.

2 oz. refined coconut oil

2 tsp. sugar

2 cups all-purpose flour.

1 tsp. kosher salt.

Directions and Ready in About: 40-Minutes.

- Blend coconut oil with salt, sugar, baking powder and flour in a food processor. Transfer this flour mixture to a mixing bowl.
- Now, add coconut milk and lemon zest to the flour mixture, then mix well. Fold in blueberries and mix the prepared dough well until smooth.
- Spread this blueberry dough into a 7-inch round and place it in a pan. Refrigerate the blueberry dough for 15 minutes, then slice it into 6 wedges.
- Layer the sheet pan with a parchment sheet. Place the blueberry wedges in the lined sheet pan. Transfer the scones to the "Ninja Foodi Digital Air Fry Oven" and close the door.
- Select *Bake* mode by rotating the dial. Press the *Time/Slice* button and change the value to 25 minutes.
- Press the *Temp/Darkness* button and change the value to 400 Degrees °F or (204 Degrees °C). Press *Start/Pause* to begin cooking. Serve fresh with blueberry jam.

Nutrition Values Per Serving: Calories: 312; Fat: 25g; Sodium: 132mg; Carbs: 44g; Fiber: 3.9g; Sugar: 3g; Protein: 1.9g

Banana Bread

Ingredients for Serving: 6

4 medium bananas, peeled and sliced.

2 large eggs

3 oz. oat flour

¾ cup sugar

½ oz. vanilla extract.

1 tsp. baking powder.

10 oz. all-purpose flour

1 tsp. baking soda

¾ cup coconut oil

¾ tsp. kosher salt.

1 cup toasted pecan.

¾ tsp. ground cinnamon.

¼ cup plain Greek yogurt

½ tsp. ground cloves

¼ tsp. ground nutmeg.

Directions and Ready in About: 40-Minutes.

- Layer a 10.5-inch-by-5.5-inch loaf pan with a parchment sheet and keep it aside. Mash the banana in a suitable bowl and add eggs, vanilla and Greek yogurt, then mix well.
- Cover this banana yogurt mixture and leave it for 30 minutes. Meanwhile, mix cinnamon, flour, sugar, baking powder, oat flour, salt, baking soda, coconut oil, cloves and nutmeg in a mixer.
- Now, slowly add banana mash mixture to the flour and continue mixing until smooth. Fold in nuts and mix gently until evenly incorporated. Spread this banana-nut batter in the prepared loaf pan.
- Transfer the loaf pan to the "Ninja Foodi Digital Air Fry Oven" and close the door. Select *Bake* mode by rotating the dial.
- Press the *Time/Slice* button and change the value to 25 minutes. Press the *Temp/Darkness* button and change the value to 350 Degrees °F or (176 Degrees °C).
- Press *Start/Pause* to begin cooking. Slice and serve with fried eggs and crispy bacon.

Nutrition Values Per Serving: Calories: 331; Fat: 2.5g; Sodium: 595mg; Carbs: 69g; Fiber: 12g; Sugar: 12g; Protein: 7g

Puffed Egg Tarts

Ingredients for Serving: 4

¾ cup Cheddar cheese, shredded.

1 tbsp. fresh parsley, minced.

½ (17.3-ounce package) frozen puff pastry, thawed

4 large eggs

Directions and Ready in About: 36-Minutes.

- Spread the pastry sheet on a floured surface and cut it into 4 squares of equal size. Place the four squares in the sheet pan of the "Ninja Foodi Digital Air Fry Oven".
- Transfer the sheet to the "Ninja Foodi Digital Air Fry Oven" and close the door. Select *Air Fry* mode by rotating the dial. Press the *Temp/Darkness* button and change the value to 300 Degrees °F or (149 Degrees °C).
- Press the *Time/Slice* button and change the value to 10 minutes, then press *Start/Pause* to begin cooking.

- Press the center of each pastry square using the back of a metal spoon.
- Divide cheese into these indentations and crack one egg into each pastry. Return to the oven and close its oven door.
- Rotate the dial to select the *Air Fry* mode. Press the *Time/Slice* button and again use the dial to set the cooking time to 11 minutes.
- Now, Press the *Temp/Darkness* button and rotate the dial to set the temperature at 350 Degrees °F or (176 Degrees °C). Garnish the squares with parsley. Serve warm with crispy bacon on the side.

Nutrition Values Per Serving: Calories: 305; Fat: 15g; Sodium: 548mg; Carbs: 26g; Fiber: 2g; Sugar: 1g; Protein: 19g

Tofu, Eggs and Mushroom Omelet

Ingredients for Serving: 2

8 oz. silken tofu, pressed, drained and crumbled.	3 eggs, beaten.
1 garlic clove, minced.	¼ onion, chopped.
3½ oz. fresh mushrooms, sliced.	2 tsp. canola oil
	Salt and ground black pepper, as needed.

Directions and Ready in About: 50-Minutes.

- In a skillet, heat the oil over medium heat and sauté the onion and garlic for about 4-5 minutes. Add the mushrooms and cook for about 4-5 minutes.
- Remove from the heat and stir in the tofu, salt and black pepper. Place the tofu mixture into a sheet pan and top with the beaten eggs.
- Press *Power* button of "Ninja Foodi Digital Air Fry Oven" and turn the dial to select *Air Fry* mode. Press *Time/Slice* button and again turn the dial to set the cooking time to 25 minutes.
- Now, push *Temp/Darkness* button and rotate the dial to set the temperature at 355 Degrees °F or (179 Degrees °C).
- Press *Start/Pause* button to start your Air Fry Oven. When the unit beeps to show that it is preheated, open the oven door.
- Arrange pan over the wire rack and insert in the oven. When cooking time is completed, open the oven door and remove the sheet pan. Cut into equal-sized wedges and serve hot alongside the greens.

Nutrition Values Per Serving: Calories: 224; Fat: 14.5g; Sat Fat: 2.9g; Carbs: 6.6g; Fiber: 0.9g; Sugar: 3.4g; Protein: 17.9g

Cheesy Toasts with Salmon

Ingredients for Serving: 2

4 oz. smoked salmon	1 tsp. lemon zest.
8 oz. ricotta cheese.	Freshly ground black pepper, to taste.
1 garlic clove, minced.	
4 bread slices	

Directions and Ready in About: 14-Minutes.

- In a food processor, add the garlic, ricotta, lemon zest and black pepper and pulse until smooth. Spread ricotta mixture over each bread slices evenly.
- Press *Power* button of "Ninja Foodi Digital Air Fry Oven" and turn the dial to select *Air Fry* mode. Press *Time/Slice* button and again turn the dial to set the cooking time to 4 minutes.
- Now, push *Temp/Darkness* button and rotate the dial to set the temperature at 355 Degrees °F or (179 Degrees °C). Press *Start/Pause* button to start your Air Fry Oven.
- When the unit beeps to show that it is preheated, open the oven door and insert the sheet pan in oven. When cooking time is completed, open the oven door and transfer the slices onto serving plates. Top with salmon and serve with the garnishing of fresh herbs.

Nutrition Values Per Serving: Calories: 274; Fat: 12g; Sat Fat: 6.3g; Carbs: 15.7g; Fiber: 0.5g; Sugar: 1.2g; Protein: 24.8g

French Toast

Ingredients for Serving: 2

4 bread slices	¼ tsp. ground turmeric
¼ cup chickpea flour.	¼ tsp. ground cumin.
3 tbsp. onion, chopped finely.	½ tsp. red chili powder
2 tsp. green chili, seeded and finely chopped.	Salt, to taste.
	Water, as needed.

Directions and Ready in About: 15-Minutes.

- Take a large bowl, add all the ingredients except bread slices and mix until a thick mixture form. With a spoon, spread the mixture over both sides of each bread slice.
- Arrange the bread slices into the lightly greased sheet pan. Press *Power* button of "Ninja Foodi Digital Air Fry Oven" and turn the dial to select *Air Fry* mode.
- Press *Time/Slice* button and again turn the dial to set the cooking time to 5 minutes. Now, push *Temp/Darkness* button and rotate the dial to set the temperature at 390 Degrees °F or (199 Degrees °C).
- Press *Start/Pause* button to start your Air Fry Oven. When the unit beeps to show that it is preheated, open the oven door and insert the sheet pan in oven.
- Flip the bread slices once halfway through. When cooking time is completed, open the oven door and serve warm with the topping of butter.

Nutrition Values Per Serving: Calories: 151; Fat: 2.3g; Sat Fat: 0.3g; Carbs: 26.7g; Fiber: 5.4g; Sugar: 4.3g; Protein: 6.5g

Raisin Bran Muffins

Ingredients for Serving: 6

4 oz. plain, non-fat Greek yogurt.	¾ oz. flaxseed
1 cup golden raisins	1 cup wheat bran
2 large eggs	1 cup boiling water
1 ½ cups whole wheat flour.	¾ cup sugar
	2 tsp. baking powder.

6 oz. butter

5 ½ oz. all-purpose flour

½ oz. ground cinnamon.

¾ tsp. kosher salt or sea salt

¼ tsp. baking soda

⅛ tsp. grated nutmeg.

Directions and Ready in About: 33-Minutes.

- Mix wheat bran with boiling water in a bowl and leave it for 5 minutes. Add eggs, wheat flour, sugar, Greek yogurt, cinnamon, salt, baking soda, baking powder, butter and nutmeg into the wheat bran, then mix well in a mixer.
- Stir in raisins and mix the batter gently. Divide this bran muffin batter into 12 greased muffin cups.
- Transfer the muffin cups to the "Ninja Foodi Digital Air Fry Oven" and close the door. Select *Bake* mode by rotating the dial.
- Press the *Time/Slice* button and change the value to 18 minutes. Press the *Temp/Darkness* button and change the value to 400 Degrees °F or (204 Degrees °C).
- Press *Start/Pause* to begin cooking. Serve fresh with caramel sauce.

Nutrition Values Per Serving: Calories: 204; Fat: 32g; Sodium: 890mg; Carbs: 4.3g; Fiber: 4g; Sugar: 8g; Protein: 5g

Mushroom Frittata

Ingredients for Serving: 4

1 shallot, sliced. thinly

½ cup cream cheese, softened

4 cups white mushrooms, chopped.

6 large eggs

2 garlic cloves, minced.

2 tbsp. olive oil

¼ tsp. red pepper flakes, crushed

½ tsp. fresh dill, minced.

Salt and ground black pepper, to taste.

Directions and Ready in About: 51-Minutes.

- In a skillet, heat the oil over medium heat and cook the shallot, mushrooms and garlic for about 5-6 minutes, stirring frequently.
- Remove from the heat and transfer the mushroom mixture into a bowl. In another bowl, add the eggs, red pepper flakes, salt and black peppers and beat well.
- Add the mushroom mixture and stir to combine. Place the egg mixture into a greased sheet pan and sprinkle with the dill.
- Spread cream cheese over egg mixture evenly. Press *Power* button of "Ninja Foodi Digital Air Fry Oven" and turn the dial to select *Air Fry* mode.
- Press *Time/Slice* button and again turn the dial to set the cooking time to 30 minutes. Now, push *Temp/Darkness* button and rotate the dial to set the temperature at 330 Degrees °F or (166 Degrees °C).
- Press *Start/Pause* button to start your Air Fry Oven. When the unit beeps to show that it is preheated, open the oven door.
- Arrange the pan over the wire rack and insert in the oven. When cooking time is completed, open the oven door and place the sheet pan onto a wire rack for about

5 minutes Cut into equal-sized wedges and serve with green salad.

Nutrition Values Per Serving: Calories: 290; Fat: 24.8g; Sat Fat: 9.7g; Carbs: 5g; Fiber: 0.8g; Sugar: 1.9g; Protein: 14.1g

Egg and Ham Cups

Ingredients for Serving: 6

6 ham slices

3 tbsp. mozzarella cheese, shredded.

6 eggs

6 tbsp. cream

¼ tsp. dried basil, crushed.

Directions and Ready in About: 28-Minutes.

- Lightly grease 6 cups of a silicone muffin tin. Line each prepared muffin cup with 1 ham slice.
- Crack 1 egg into each muffin cup and top with cream. Sprinkle with cheese and basil. Press *Power* button of "Ninja Foodi Digital Air Fry Oven" and turn the dial to select *Air Fry* mode.
- Press *Time/Slice* button and again turn the dial to set the cooking time to 18 minutes. Now, push *Temp/Darkness* button and rotate the dial to set the temperature at 350 Degrees °F or (176 Degrees °C).
- Press *Start/Pause* button to start your Air Fry Oven. When the unit beeps to show that it is preheated, open the oven door. Arrange the muffin tin over the wire rack and insert in the oven.
- When cooking time is completed, open the oven door and place the muffin tin onto a wire rack to cool for about 5 minutes. Carefully invert the muffins onto the platter and serve warm. alongside the buttered bread slices.

Nutrition Values Per Serving: Calories: 156; Fat: 10g; Sat Fat: 4.1g; Carbs: 2.3g; Fiber: 0.4g; Sugar: 0.6g; Protein: 14.3g

Spiced and Sweet Toasts

Ingredients for Serving: 3

6 bread slices.

¼ cup salted butter, softened

¼ cup sugar

½ tsp. ground cinnamon.

⅛ tsp. ground cloves

⅛ tsp. ground ginger.

½ tsp. vanilla extract

Pepper, as you need.

Directions and Ready in About: 14-Minutes.

- Take a bowl, add the sugar, vanilla, cinnamon, pepper and butter. Mix until smooth. Spread the butter mixture evenly over each bread slice.
- Press *Power* button of "Ninja Foodi Digital Air Fry Oven" and turn the dial to select *Air Fry* mode.
- Press *Time/Slice* button and again turn the dial to set the cooking time to 4 minutes. Now, push *Temp/Darkness* button and rotate the dial to set the temperature at 400 Degrees °F or (204 Degrees °C).
- Press *Start/Pause* button to start your Air Fry Oven. When the unit beeps to show that it is preheated, open the oven door and grease the air fry basket.
- Place the bread slices into the prepared air fry basket, buttered-side up and insert in the oven.

- Flip the slices once halfway through. When cooking time is completed, open the oven door and transfer the French toasts onto a platter. Serve warm with the drizzling of maple syrup.

Nutrition Values Per Serving: Calories: 261; Fat: 12g; Sat Fat: 3.6g; Carbs: 30.6g; Fiber: 0.3g; Sugar: 22.3g; Protein: 9.1g

Mushrooms Frittata

Ingredients for Serving: 2

¼ cup mushrooms, sliced.	2 tbsp. skim milk
¼ cup tomato, sliced.	2 tbsp. fresh chives, chopped.
1 cup egg whites	Black pepper, to taste.

Directions and Ready in About: 30-Minutes.

- Beat egg whites with mushrooms and the rest of the ingredients in a bowl. Spread this egg white mixture in a suitable casserole dish.
- Transfer the dish to the "Ninja Foodi Digital Air Fry Oven" and close the door. Select *Air Fry* mode by rotating the dial.
- Press the *Time/Slice* button and change the value to 15 minutes. Press the *Temp/Darkness* button and change the value to 320 Degrees °F or (160 Degrees °C).
- Press *Start/Pause* to begin cooking. Slice and serve warm with crispy bacon on the side.

Nutrition Values Per Serving: Calories: 354; Fat: 7.9g; Sodium: 704mg; Carbs: 6g; Fiber: 3.6g; Sugar: 6g; Protein: 18g

Instant Easy Bread

Ingredients for Serving: 4

1¾ oz. pumpkin seeds	⅞ cup plain flour.
⅞ cup whole-wheat flour.	½ of sachet instant yeast
½-1 cup lukewarm water	1 tsp. salt

Directions and Ready in About: 33-Minutes.

- Take a bowl, mix the flours, pumpkin seeds, salt and yeast and mix well together. Slowly, add the desired amount of water and mix until a soft dough ball forms.
- With your hands, knead the dough until smooth and elastic. Place the dough ball into a bowl. With a plastic wrap, cover the bowl and set aside in a warm place for 30 minutes or until doubled in size.
- Press *Power* button of "Ninja Foodi Digital Air Fry Oven" and turn the dial to select *Air Fry* mode. Press *Time/Slice* button and again turn the dial to set the cooking time to 18 minutes.
- Now, push *Temp/Darkness* button and rotate the dial to set the temperature at 350 Degrees °F or (176 Degrees °C). Press *Start/Pause* button to start your Air Fry Oven.
- Place the dough ball in a greased sheet pan and brush the top of the dough with water. When the unit beeps to show that it is preheated, open the oven door.
- Place the sheet pan into the air fry basket and insert in the oven. When cooking time is completed, open the

oven door and place the pan onto a wire rack for about 10-15 minutes.
- Carefully, invert the bread onto the wire rack to cool completely cool before slicing. Cut the bread into desired sized slices and serve with your favorite jam.

Nutrition Values Per Serving: Calories: 268; Fat: 6g; Sat Fat: 1.1g; Carbs: 43.9g; Fiber: 2.5g; Sugar: 1.1g; Protein: 9.2g

Carrot and Raisin Bread

Ingredients for Serving: 8

2 cups all-purpose flour	½ cup applesauce.
3 eggs	¼ cup honey
½ cup sunflower oil	¼ cup plain yogurt
2½ cups carrots, peeled and shredded.	1½ tsp. ground cinnamon.
	2 tsp. vanilla essence
½ cup raisins	2 tsp. baking soda.
½ cup walnuts	½ tsp. salt

Directions and Ready in About: 50-Minutes.

- Line the bottom of a greased baking pan with parchment paper. Take a medium bowl, sift together the flour, baking soda, cinnamon and salt.
- Take a large bowl, add the eggs, oil, applesauce, honey and yogurt and with a hand-held mixer, mix on medium speed until well combined.
- Add the eggs, one at a time and whisk well. Add the vanilla and mix well. Add the flour mixture and mix until just combined.
- Fold in the carrots, raisins and walnuts. Place the mixture into a lightly greased baking pan. With a piece of foil, cover the pan loosely.
- Press *Power* button of "Ninja Foodi Digital Air Fry Oven" and turn the dial to select the *Air Fry* mode.
- Press *Time/Slice* button and again turn the dial to set the cooking time to 30 minutes. Now, push *Temp/Darkness* button and rotate the dial to set the temperature at 350 Degrees °F or (176 Degrees °C).
- Press *Start/Pause* button to start your Air Fry Oven. When the unit beeps to show that it is preheated, open the oven door.
- Arrange the pan into the air fry basket and insert in the oven. After 25 minutes of cooking, remove the foil.
- When cooking time is completed, open the oven door and place the pan onto a wire rack to cool for about 10 minutes. Carefully invert the bread onto the wire rack to cool completely before slicing. Cut the bread into desired-sized slices and serve with butter.

Nutrition Values Per Serving: Calories: 441; Fat: 20.3g; Sat Fat: 2.2g; Carbs: 57.6g; Fiber: 5.7g; Sugar: 23.7g; Protein: 9.2g

Savory Beans and Sausage Muffins

Ingredients for Serving: 6

½ cup cheddar cheese, shredded.	3 tbsp. heavy cream.
	1 tbsp. tomato paste
4 eggs	¼ tsp. salt

4 cooked breakfast sausage links, chopped.

3 tbsp. baked beans

Cooking spray

Pinch of freshly ground black pepper.

Directions and Ready in About: 35-Minutes.

- Grease a 6-cup muffin pan. Take a bowl, add the eggs, cheddar cheese, heavy cream, tomato paste, salt and black pepper and beat until well combined.
- Stir in the sausage pieces and beans. Divide the mixture into prepared muffin cups evenly. Press *Power* button of "Ninja Foodi Digital Air Fry Oven" and turn the dial to select *Bake* mode.
- Press *Time/Slice* button and again turn the dial to set the cooking time to 20 minutes. Now, push *Temp/Darkness* button and rotate the dial to set the temperature at 350 Degrees °F or (176 Degrees °C).
- Press *Start/Pause* button to start your Air Fry Oven. When the unit beeps to show that it is preheated, open the oven door.
- Arrange the muffin pan over the wire rack and insert in the oven. When cooking time is completed, open the oven door and place the muffin pan onto a wire rack to cool for 5 minutes before serving with drizzling of melted butter.

Nutrition Values Per Serving: Calories: 258; Fat: 20.4g; Sat Fat: 9.3g; Carbs: 4.2g; Fiber: 0.8g; Sugar: 0.9g; Protein: 14.6g

Cloud Eggs Breakfast

Ingredients for Serving: 2

2 eggs, whites and yolks separated.

Pinch of salt.

Pinch of freshly ground black pepper

Directions and Ready in About: 17-Minutes.

- Take a bowl, add the egg white, salt and black pepper and beat until stiff peaks form. Line a baking pan with parchment paper.
- Carefully, make a pocket in the center of each egg white circle. Press *Power* button of "Ninja Foodi Digital Air Fry Oven" and turn the dial to select the "Air Broil" mode.
- Press *Time/Slice* button and again turn the dial to set the cooking time to 7 minutes.
- Press *Temp/Darkness* button and again turn the dial to set LO. To set the temperature, press the *Temp/Darkness* button again.
- When the unit beeps to show that it is preheated, open the oven door and insert the sheet pan in the oven. Place 1 egg yolk into each egg white pocket after 5 minutes of cooking.
- Press *Start/Pause* button to start your Air Fry Oven. When cooking time is completed, open the oven door and serve alongside toasted bread slices.

Nutrition Values Per Serving: Calories: 63; Fat: 4.4g; Sat Fat: 1.4g; Carbs: 0.3g; Fiber: 0g; Sugar: 0.3g; Protein: 5.5g

Healthy Date Bread

Ingredients for Serving: 10

2½ cups dates, pitted and chopped.

½ cup brown sugar

1½ cups flour.

¼ cup butter

1 cup hot water.

1 egg

1 tsp. baking powder.

1 tsp. baking soda

½ tsp. salt

Directions and Ready in About: 37-Minutes.

- Take a large bowl, add the dates and butter and top with the hot water. Set aside for about 5 minutes. In a separate bowl, mix the flour, brown sugar, baking powder, baking soda and salt together.
- In the same bowl of dates, add the flour mixture and egg and mix well. Grease a non-stick loaf pan. Place the mixture into the prepared pan.
- Press *Power* button of "Ninja Foodi Digital Air Fry Oven" and turn the dial to select *Air Fry* mode. Press *Time/Slice* button and again turn the dial to set the cooking time to 22 minutes.
- Now, push *Temp/Darkness* button and rotate the dial to set the temperature at 340 Degrees °F or (171 Degrees °C). Press *Start/Pause* button to start your Air Fry Oven.
- When the unit beeps to show that it is preheated, open the oven door. Place the pan into the air fry basket and insert in the oven.
- When cooking time is completed, open the oven door and place the pan onto a wire rack for about 10-15 minutes. Carefully, invert the bread onto the wire rack to cool completely cool before slicing.
- Cut the bread into desired sized slices and serve these bread slices with butter.

Nutrition Values Per Serving: Calories: 129; Fat: 5.4g; Sat Fat: 3.1g; Carbs: 55.1g; Fiber: 4.1g; Sugar: 35.3g; Protein: 3.6g

Poultry Recipes

Bacon Wrapped Chicken Breasts

Ingredients for Serving: 2

2 (5- to 6-ounce) boneless, skinless chicken breasts.

4 thin bacon slices

½ tsp. garlic powder.

½ tsp. smoked paprika

Salt and ground black pepper, to taste.

Directions and Ready in About: 45-Minutes.

- With a meat mallet, lb. each chicken breast into ¾-inch thickness. Take a bowl, mix together the paprika, garlic powder, salt and black pepper.
- Rub the chicken breasts with spice mixture evenly. Wrap each chicken breast with bacon strips.
- Press *Power* button of "Ninja Foodi Digital Air Fry Oven" and turn the dial to select *Air Fry* mode. Press *Time/Slice* button and again turn the dial to set the cooking time to 35 minutes.
- Now, push *Temp/Darkness* button and rotate the dial to set the temperature at 400 Degrees °F or (204 Degrees °C).
- Press *Start/Pause* button to start your Air Fry Oven. When the unit beeps to show that it is preheated, open the oven door.
- Arrange the chicken pieces into the greased air fry basket and insert in the oven. Once the cooking time is completed, open the oven door and serve hot with fresh baby greens.

Nutrition Values Per Serving: Calories: 293; Fat: 17.4g; Sat Fat: 5.4g; Carbs: 0.8g; Fiber: 0.1g; Sugar: 0.1g; Protein: 31.3g

Parmesan Chicken Tenders

Ingredients for Serving: 4

8 chicken tenders.

¾ cup Parmesan cheese, grated finely

¾ cup panko breadcrumbs.

2 eggs, beaten.

½ cup flour

1 tsp. Italian seasoning

Salt and ground black pepper, to taste.

Directions and Ready in About: 30-Minutes.

- In a shallow dish, mix together the flour, salt and black pepper. In a second shallow dish, place the beaten eggs.
- In a third shallow dish, mix together the breadcrumbs, parmesan cheese and Italian seasoning.
- Coat the chicken tenders with flour mixture, then dip into the beaten eggs and finally coat with breadcrumb mixture.
- Arrange the tenders onto a greased sheet pan in a single layer. Press *Power* button of "Ninja Foodi Digital Air Fry Oven" and turn the dial to select *Air Fry* mode.
- Press *Time/Slice* button and again turn the dial to set the cooking time to 15 minutes.
- Now, push *Temp/Darkness* button and rotate the dial to set the temperature at 360 Degrees °F or (182 Degrees

°C). Press *Start/Pause* button to start your Air Fry Oven.

- When the unit beeps to show that it is preheated, open the oven door and insert the sheet pan in oven. Once the cooking time is completed, open the oven door and serve hot with blue cheese dip.

Nutrition Values Per Serving: Calories: 435; Fat: 16.1g; Sat Fat: 5.4g; Carbs: 15.3g; Fiber: 0g; Sugar: 0.5g; Protein: 0.4g

Buttermilk Whole Chicken

Ingredients for Serving: 6

1 (3-pound) whole chicken, neck and giblets removed.

2 cups buttermilk

¼ cup olive oil.

1 tsp. garlic powder

Ground black pepper, to taste.

Salt, to taste.

Directions and Ready in About: 1 hr. 5-Minutes.

- In a large resealable bag, mix together the buttermilk, oil, garlic powder and 1 tbsp. of salt. Add the whole chicken and seal the bag tightly.
- Refrigerate to marinate for 24 hours up to 2 days. Remove the chicken from bag and pat dry with paper towels. Season the chicken with salt and black pepper. With kitchen twine, tie off wings and legs.
- Press *Power* button of "Ninja Foodi Digital Air Fry Oven" and turn the dial to select *Air Fry* mode. Press *Time/Slice* button and again turn the dial to set the cooking time to 50 minutes.
- Now, push *Temp/Darkness* button and rotate the dial to set the temperature at 380 Degrees °F or (193 Degrees °C). Press *Start/Pause* button to start your Air Fry Oven. When the unit beeps to show that it is preheated, open the oven door.
- Arrange the chicken into the greased air fry basket, breast-side down and insert in the oven. Once the cooking time is completed, open the oven door and place the chicken onto a cutting board for about 10 minutes before carving.
- With a sharp knife, cut the chicken into desired sized pieces and serve with steamed veggies.

Nutrition Values Per Serving: Calories: 449; Fat: 16g; Sat Fat: 3.6g; Carbs: 68.5g; Fiber: 4.3g; Sugar: 0.1g; Protein: 4g

Lemony Chicken Thighs

Ingredients for Serving: 6

6 (6-ounce) chicken thighs.

1 lemon, sliced. thinly

1 tbsp. Italian seasoning.

2 tbsp. olive oil

2 tbsp. fresh lemon juice

Salt and ground black pepper, to taste.

Directions and Ready in About: 35-Minutes.

- Take a large bowl, add all the ingredients except for lemon slices and toss to coat well. Refrigerate to marinate for 30 minutes to overnight. Remove the chicken thighs from bowl and let any excess marinade drip off.

- Press *Power* button of "Ninja Foodi Digital Air Fry Oven" and turn the dial to select *Air Fry* mode. Press *Time/Slice* button and again turn the dial to set the cooking time to 20 minutes.
- Now, push *Temp/Darkness* button and rotate the dial to set the temperature at 350 Degrees °F or (176 Degrees °C).
- Press *Start/Pause* button to start your Air Fry Oven. When the unit beeps to show that it is preheated, open the oven door.
- Arrange the chicken thighs into the greased air fry basket and insert the basket in oven. Flip the chicken thighs once halfway through.
- Once the cooking time is completed, open the oven door and serve hot alongside the lemon slices and with your favorite salad.

Nutrition Values Per Serving: Calories: 372; Fat: 18g; Sat Fat: 4.3g; Carbs: 0.6g; Fiber: 0.1g; Sugar: 0.4g; Protein: 49.3g

Lemony Whole Chicken

Ingredients for Serving: 8

1 (5-pound) whole chicken, neck and giblets removed.

1 small onion, peeled and quartered

1 garlic clove, peeled and cut in half.

2 fresh rosemary sprigs

4 lemon zest slices

1 tbsp. extra-virgin olive oil.

1 tbsp. fresh lemon juice

Salt and ground black pepper, to taste.

Directions and Ready in About: 1 hr. 35-Minutes.

- Rub the inside and outside of chicken with salt and black pepper evenly. Place the rosemary sprigs, onion quarters, garlic halves and lemon zest in the cavity of the chicken.
- With kitchen twine, tie off wings and legs. Arrange the chicken onto a greased sheet pan and drizzle with oil and lemon juice.
- Press *Power* button of "Ninja Foodi Digital Air Fry Oven" and turn the dial to select *Bake* mode. Press *Time/Slice* button and again turn the dial to set the cooking time to 20 minutes.
- Now, push *Temp/Darkness* button and rotate the dial to set the temperature at 400 Degrees °F or (204 Degrees °C).
- Press *Start/Pause* button to start your Air Fry Oven. When the unit beeps to show that it is preheated, open the oven door.
- Arrange the pan over the wire rack and insert in the oven. After 20 minutes of cooking, set the temperature to 375 Degrees °F or (190 Degrees °C) for 60 minutes.
- When cooking time is completed, open the oven door and place the chicken onto a platter for about 10 minutes before carving. Cut into desired sized pieces and serve alongside with the steamed veggies.

Nutrition Values Per Serving: Calories: 448; Fat: 10.4g; Sat Fat: 2.7g; Carbs: 1g; Fiber: 0.4g; Sugar: 0.2g; Protein: 82g

Cajun Spiced Whole Chicken

Ingredients for Serving: 6

1 (3-pound) whole chicken, neck and giblets removed.

¼ cup butter, softened

1 tbsp. garlic powder.

1 tbsp. Cajun seasoning

1 tbsp. paprika

1 tbsp. onion powder.

2 tsp. dried rosemary

2 tsp. dried thyme

1 tsp. cayenne pepper.

Salt, to taste.

Directions and Ready in About: 1 hr. 25-Minutes.

- Take a bowl, add the butter, herbs, spices and salt and mix well. Rub the chicken with spicy mixture generously. With kitchen twine, tie off wings and legs.
- Press *Power* button of "Ninja Foodi Digital Air Fry Oven" and turn the dial to select *Bake* mode. Press *Time/Slice* button and again turn the dial to set the cooking time to 70 minutes.
- Now, push *Temp/Darkness* button and rotate the dial to set the temperature at 380 Degrees °F or (193 Degrees °C). Press *Start/Pause* button to start your Air Fry Oven. When the unit beeps to show that it is preheated, open the oven door.
- Arrange the chicken over the wire rack and insert in the oven. When cooking time is completed, open the oven door and place the chicken onto a platter for about 10 minutes before carving. Cut into desired sized pieces and serve alongside with a fresh green salad.

Nutrition Values Per Serving: Calories: 421; Fat: 14.8g; Sat Fat: 6.9g; Carbs: 2.3g; Fiber: 0.9g; Sugar: 0.5g; Protein: 66.3g

Molasses Glazed Duck Breast

Ingredients for Serving: 3

1 lb. boneless duck breast.

2 cups fresh pomegranate juice

3 tbsp. brown sugar.

2 tbsp. fresh lemon juice

Salt and ground black pepper, to taste.

Directions and Ready in About: 1 hr.

- For pomegranate molasses: in a medium saucepan, add the pomegranate juice, lemon and brown sugar over medium heat and bring to a boil.
- Reduce the heat to low and simmer for about 25 minutes until the mixture is thick. Remove from the hat and set aside to cool slightly.
- Meanwhile, with a knife, make the slit on the duck breast. Season the duck breast with salt and black pepper generously.
- Press *Power* button of "Ninja Foodi Digital Air Fry Oven" and turn the dial to select *Air Fry* mode. Press *Time/Slice* button and again turn the dial to set the cooking time to 14 minutes.
- Now, push *Temp/Darkness* button and rotate the dial to set the temperature at 400 Degrees °F or (204 Degrees °C). Press *Start/Pause* button to start your Air Fry Oven.

- When the unit beeps to show that it is preheated, open the oven door. Arrange the duck breast into the greased air fry basket, skin side up and insert in the oven.
- After 6 minutes of cooking, flip the duck breast. Once the cooking time is completed, open the oven door and place the duck breast onto a platter for about 5 minutes before slicing.
- With a sharp knife, cut the duck breast into desired sized slices and transfer onto a platter. Drizzle with warm molasses and serve alongside with the garlicky sweet potatoes.

Nutrition Values Per Serving: Calories: 332; Fat: 6.1g; Sat Fat: 0.1g; Carbs: 337g; Fiber: 0g; Sugar: 31.6g; Protein: 34g

Baked Chicken Thighs

Ingredients for Serving: 4

4 (4-ounce) skinless, boneless chicken thighs.	Salt and ground black pepper, to taste.
2 tbsp. butter, melted	

Directions and Ready in About: 30-Minutes.

- Line a sheet pan with a lightly greased piece of foil. Rub the chicken thighs with salt and black pepper evenly and then, brush with melted butter. Place the chicken thighs into the prepared sheet pan.
- Press *Power* button of "Ninja Foodi Digital Air Fry Oven" and turn the dial to select *Bake* mode. Press *Time/Slice* button and again turn the dial to set the cooking time to 20 minutes.
- Now, push *Temp/Darkness* button and rotate the dial to set the temperature at 450 Degrees °F or (232 Degrees °C).
- Press *Start/Pause* button to start your Air Fry Oven. When the unit beeps to show that it is preheated, open the oven door and insert the sheet pan in oven. Once the cooking time is completed, open the oven door and serve hot alongside with the creamy mashed potatoes.

Nutrition Values Per Serving: Calories: 193; Fat: 9.8g; Sat Fat: 5.2g; Carbs: 0g; Fiber: 0g; Sugar: 0g; Protein: 25.4g

Crispy Roasted Chicken

Ingredients for Serving: 8

1 (3½-pound) whole chicken, cut into 8 pieces.	1 tbsp. paprika.
2 cups all-purpose flour	1 tbsp. ground mustard
2 cups buttermilk.	1 tbsp. garlic powder
1 tbsp. onion powder	Salt and ground black pepper, to taste.

Directions and Ready in About: 55-Minutes.

- Rub the chicken pieces with salt and black pepper. Take a large bowl, add the chicken pieces and buttermilk and refrigerate to marinate for at least 1 hour.
- Meanwhile, in a large bowl, place the flour, mustard, spices, salt and black pepper and mix well. Remove the chicken pieces from bowl and drip off the excess buttermilk. Coat the chicken pieces with the flour mixture, shaking any excess off.

- Press *Power* button of "Ninja Foodi Digital Air Fry Oven" and turn the dial to select *Air Fry* mode. Press *Time/Slice* button and again turn the dial to set the cooking time to 20 minutes.
- Now, push *Temp/Darkness* button and rotate the dial to set the temperature at 390 Degrees °F or (199 Degrees °C).
- Press *Start/Pause* button to start your Air Fry Oven. When the unit beeps to show that it is preheated, open the oven door and grease air fry basket.
- Arrange half of the chicken pieces into air fry basket and insert in the oven. Repeat with the remaining chicken pieces. Once the cooking time is completed, open the oven door and serve immediately alongside with the French fries.

Nutrition Values Per Serving: Calories: 518; Fat: 8.5g; Sat Fat: 2.4g; Carbs: 33.4g; Fiber: 1.8|Sugar: 4.3g; Protein: 72.6g

Crispy Chicken Drumsticks

Ingredients for Serving: 4

4 chicken drumsticks.	½ tbsp. paprika.
¼ cup cornstarch	2 tbsp. milk
1 cup all-purpose flour.	1 tbsp. adobo seasoning.
2 eggs	Ground black pepper, to taste.
1 tbsp. onion powder.	
1 tbsp. garlic powder	Salt, to taste.

Directions and Ready in About: 40-Minutes.

- Season chicken drumsticks with adobo seasoning and a pinch of salt. Set aside for about 5minutes.
- Take a small bowl, add the spices, salt and black pepper and mix well. Take a shallow bowl, add the eggs, milk and 1 tsp. of spice mixture and beat until well combined.
- In another shallow bowl, add the flour, cornstarch and remaining spice mixture. Coat the chicken drumsticks with flour mixture and tap off the excess.
- Now, dip the chicken drumsticks in egg mixture. Again coat the chicken drumsticks with flour mixture. Arrange the chicken drumsticks onto a wire rack lined baking sheet and set aside for about 15 minutes.
- Now, arrange the chicken drumsticks onto a sheet pan and spray the chicken with cooking spray lightly.
- Press *Power* button of "Ninja Foodi Digital Air Fry Oven" and turn the dial to select *Air Fry* mode. Press *Time/Slice* button and again turn the dial to set the cooking time to 25 minutes.
- Now, push *Temp/Darkness* button and rotate the dial to set the temperature at 350 Degrees °F or (176 Degrees °C).
- Press *Start/Pause* button to start your Air Fry Oven. When the unit beeps to show that it is preheated, open the oven door and grease the air fry basket.
- Place the chicken drumsticks into the prepared air fry basket and insert in the oven. When cooking time is completed, open the oven door and serve hot with French fries.

Brie Stuffed Chicken Breasts

Ingredients for Serving: 4

2 (8-ounce) skinless, boneless chicken fillets.

4 bacon slices

4 brie cheese slices.

1 tbsp. fresh chive, minced.

Salt and ground black pepper, to taste.

Directions and Ready in About: 30-Minutes.

- Cut each chicken fillet in 2 equal-sized pieces. Carefully, make a slit in each chicken piece horizontally about ¼-inch from the edge.
- Open each chicken piece and season with salt and black pepper. Place 1 cheese slice in the open area of each chicken piece and sprinkle with chives. Close the chicken pieces and wrap each one with a bacon slice.
- Secure with toothpicks. Press *Power* button of "Ninja Foodi Digital Air Fry Oven" and turn the dial to select *Air Fry* mode.
- Press *Time/Slice* button and again turn the dial to set the cooking time to 15 minutes. Now, push *Temp/Darkness* button and rotate the dial to set the temperature at 355 Degrees °F or (179 Degrees °C).
- Press *Start/Pause* button to start your Air Fry Oven. When the unit beeps to show that it is preheated, open the oven door and grease the air fry basket. Place the chicken pieces into the prepared air fry basket and insert in the oven.
- When cooking time is completed, open the oven door and place the rolled chicken breasts onto a cutting board. Cut into desired-sized slices and serve with creamy mashed potatoes.

Parmesan Crusted Chicken Breasts

Ingredients for Serving: 4

2 large chicken breasts.

1 cup panko breadcrumbs

1 cup mayonnaise

1 cup Parmesan cheese, shredded.

Directions and Ready in About: 30-Minutes.

- Cut each chicken breast in half and then with a meat mallet lb. each into even thickness. Spread the mayonnaise on both sides of each chicken piece evenly.
- Take a shallow bowl, mix together the Parmesan and breadcrumbs. Coat the chicken piece Parmesan mixture evenly.
- Press *Power* button of "Ninja Foodi Digital Air Fry Oven" and turn the dial to select *Air Fry* mode. Press *Time/Slice* button and again turn the dial to set the cooking time to 15 minutes.
- Now, push *Temp/Darkness* button and rotate the dial to set the temperature at 390 Degrees °F or (199 Degrees °C).

- Press *Start/Pause* button to start your Air Fry Oven. When the unit beeps to show that it is preheated, open the oven door.
- Arrange the chicken pieces into the greased air fry basket and insert in the oven. After 10 minutes of cooking, flip the chicken pieces once. Once the cooking time is completed, open the oven door and serve hot with ranch dip.

Spiced Chicken Breasts

Ingredients for Serving: 4

2 (12-ounce) chicken breasts.

1 tsp. ground cumin

1½ tbsp. smoked paprika.

1 tbsp. olive oil

Salt and ground black pepper, to taste.

Directions and Ready in About: 45-Minutes.

- Take a small bowl, mix together the paprika, cumin, salt and black pepper. Coat the chicken breasts with oil evenly and then season with the spice mixture generously.
- Press *Power* button of "Ninja Foodi Digital Air Fry Oven" and turn the dial to select *Air Fry* mode. Press *Time/Slice* button and again turn the dial to set the cooking time to 35 minutes.
- Now, push *Temp/Darkness* button and rotate the dial to set the temperature at 375 Degrees °F or (190 Degrees °C).
- Press *Start/Pause* button to start your Air Fry Oven. When the unit beeps to show that it is preheated, open the oven door. Arrange the peanuts into the air fry basket and insert in the oven.
- Once the cooking time is completed, open the oven door and place the chicken breasts onto a cutting board for about 5 minutes. Cut each breast in 2 equal-sized pieces and serve with sautéed kale.

Chinese Style Chicken Drumsticks

Ingredients for Serving: 4

4 (6-ounce) chicken drumsticks.

1 cup cornflour

1 tsp. Chinese five-spice powder

1 tbsp. oyster sauce.

1 tsp. light soy sauce.

½ tsp. sesame oil

Salt and ground white pepper, to taste.

Directions and Ready in About: 30-Minutes.

- Take a bowl, mix together the sauces, oil, five-spice powder, salt and black pepper. Add the chicken drumsticks and generously coat with the marinade. Refrigerate for at least 30-40 minutes.
- In a shallow dish, place the Cornflour. Remove the chicken from marinade and lightly coat with cornflour.

- Press *Power* button of "Ninja Foodi Digital Air Fry Oven" and turn the dial to select *Air Fry* mode. Press *Time/Slice* button and again turn the dial to set the cooking time to 20 minutes.
- Now, push *Temp/Darkness* button and rotate the dial to set the temperature at 390 Degrees °F or (199 Degrees °C).
- Press *Start/Pause* button to start your Air Fry Oven. When the unit beeps to show that it is preheated, open the oven door and grease the air fry basket.
- Place the chicken drumsticks into the prepared air fry basket and insert in the oven. When cooking time is completed, open the oven door and serve hot with fresh greens.

Nutrition Values Per Serving: Calories: 287; Fat: 13.8g; Sat Fat: 7.1g; Carbs: 1.6g; Fiber: 0.2g; Sugar: 0.1g; Protein: 38.3g

Primavera Chicken

Ingredients for Serving: 4

4 chicken breasts, boneless	2 tbsp. olive oil
3 medium tomatoes, sliced.	1 tsp. Italian seasoning
2 yellow bell peppers, sliced.	Kosher salt, to taste.
½ red onion, sliced.	Freshly chopped parsley for garnish
1 cup shredded mozzarella	Freshly ground black pepper, to taste.
1 zucchini, sliced.	

Directions and Ready in About: 40-Minutes.

- Carve one side slit in the chicken breasts and stuff them with all the veggies. Place these stuffed chicken breasts in a casserole dish, then drizzle oil, Italian seasoning, black pepper, salt and Mozzarella over the chicken.
- Transfer the dish to the "Ninja Foodi Digital Air Fry Oven" and close the door. Select *Bake* mode by rotating the dial.
- Press the *Time/Slice* button and change the value to 25 minutes. Press the *Temp/Darkness* button and change the value to 370 Degrees °F or (187 Degrees °C).
- Press *Start/Pause* to begin cooking. Garnish with parsley and serve warm with a kale salad on the side.

Nutrition Values Per Serving: Calories: 445; Fat: 25g; Sodium: 122mg; Carbs: 13g; Fiber: 0.4g; Sugar: 1g; Protein: 33g

Deviled Chicken

Ingredients for Serving: 8

8 small bone-in chicken thighs, skin removed.	¼ cup chives, chopped.
1 cup Dijon mustard	2 cloves garlic, chopped.
1 ½ cups panko breadcrumbs.	2 tbsp. butter
¾ cup Parmesan, freshly grated	½ tsp. cayenne pepper.
	2 tsp. paprika

Directions and Ready in About: 55-Minutes.

- Toss the chicken thighs with crumbs, cheese, chives, butter and spices in a bowl and mix well to coat. Transfer the chicken along with its spice mix to a sheet pan.
- Transfer the pan to the "Ninja Foodi Digital Air Fry Oven" and close the door.
- Select *Air Fry* mode by rotating the dial. Press the *Time/Slice* button and change the value to 40 minutes.
- Press the *Temp/Darkness* button and change the value to 375 Degrees °F or (190 Degrees °C). Press *Start/Pause* to begin cooking. Serve warm chicken fried rice or sautéed vegetable.

Nutrition Values Per Serving: Calories: 497; Fat: 14g; Sodium: 364mg; Carbs: 8g; Fiber: 1g; Sugar: 3g; Protein: 32g

Fried Turkey Wings

Ingredients for Serving: 4

2 lbs. turkey wings.	4 tbsp. chicken rub
3 tbsp. olive oil	

Directions and Ready in About: 36-Minutes.

- Take a large bowl, add the turkey wings, chicken rub and olive oil and toss to coat well.
- Press *Power* button of "Ninja Foodi Digital Air Fry Oven" and turn the dial to select *Air Fry* mode. Press *Time/Slice* button and again turn the dial to set the cooking time to 26 minutes.
- Now, push *Temp/Darkness* button and rotate the dial to set the temperature at 380 Degrees °F or (193 Degrees °C).
- Press *Start/Pause* button to start your Air Fry Oven. When the unit beeps to show that it is preheated, open the oven door.
- Arrange the turkey wings into the greased air fry basket and insert in the oven. Flip the turkey wings once halfway through. Once the cooking time is completed, open the oven door and serve hot alongside with the yogurt sauce.

Nutrition Values Per Serving: Calories: 558; Fat: 38.9g; Sat Fat: 1.5g; Carbs: 3g; Fiber: 0g; Sugar: 0g; Protein: 46.6g

Herbed Chicken Thighs

Ingredients for Serving: 4

4 (5-ounce) chicken thighs.	2 tbsp. olive oil
½ tbsp. fresh rosemary, minced.	Salt and ground black pepper, to taste.
½ tbsp. fresh thyme, minced.	

Directions and Ready in About: 30-Minutes.

- Take a large bowl, add the herbs, salt and black pepper and mix well. Coat the chicken thighs with oil and then, rub with herb mixture. Arrange the chicken thighs onto the greased sheet pan.
- Press *Power* button of "Ninja Foodi Digital Air Fry Oven" and turn the dial to select *Air Fry* mode. Press *Time/Slice* button and again turn the dial to set the cooking time to 20 minutes.

- Now, push *Temp/Darkness* button and rotate the dial to set the temperature at 400 Degrees °F or (204 Degrees °C).
- Press *Start/Pause* button to start your Air Fry Oven. When the unit beeps to show that it is preheated, open the oven door and insert the sheet pan in oven.
- Flip the chicken thighs once halfway through. Once the cooking time is completed, open the oven door and serve hot with couscous salad.

Nutrition Values Per Serving: Calories: 332; Fat: 17.6g; Sat Fat: 2.9g; Carbs: 0.5g; Fiber: 0.3g; Sugar: 0g; Protein: 41.1g

Herbed Duck Breast

Ingredients for Serving: 2

1 (10-ounce) duck breast.

1 cup chicken broth

1 tbsp. fresh lemon juice

½ tbsp. fresh thyme, chopped.

½ tbsp. fresh rosemary, chopped.

Salt and ground black pepper, to taste.

Olive oil cooking spray

Directions and Ready in About: 35-Minutes.

- Spray the duck breast with cooking spray evenly. Take a bowl, mix well the remaining ingredients. Add the duck breast and coat with the marinade generously. Refrigerate, covered for about 4 hours. With a piece of foil, cover the duck breast.
- Press *Power* button of "Ninja Foodi Digital Air Fry Oven" and turn the dial to select *Air Fry* mode. Press *Time/Slice* button and again turn the dial to set the cooking time to 15 minutes.
- Now, push *Temp/Darkness* button and rotate the dial to set the temperature at 390 Degrees °F or (199 Degrees °C). Press *Start/Pause* button to start your Air Fry Oven.
- When the unit beeps to show that it is preheated, open the oven door and grease the air fry basket. Place the duck breast into the prepared air fry basket and insert in the oven.
- After 15 minutes of cooking, set the temperature to 355 Degrees °F or (179 Degrees °C) for 5 minutes. When cooking time is completed, open the oven door and serve hot with spiced potatoes.

Nutrition Values Per Serving: Calories: 209; Fat: 6.6g; Sat Fat: 0.3g; Carbs: 1.6g; Fiber: 0.6g; Sugar: 0.5g; Protein: 33.8g

Oat Crusted Chicken Breasts

Ingredients for Serving: 2

2 (6-ounce) chicken breasts.

2 medium eggs

¾ cup oats

2 tbsp. mustard powder.

1 tbsp. fresh parsley

Salt and ground black pepper, to taste.

Directions and Ready in About: 27-Minutes.

- Place the chicken breasts onto a cutting board and with a meat mallet, flatten each into even thickness. Then, cut each breast in half. Sprinkle the chicken pieces with salt and black pepper and set aside.

- In a blender, add the oats, mustard powder, parsley, salt and black pepper and pulse until a coarse breadcrumb-like mixture is formed.
- Transfer the oat mixture into a shallow bowl. In another bowl, crack the eggs and beat well. Coat the chicken with oats mixture and then, dip into beaten eggs and again, coat with the oats mixture.
- Press *Power* button of "Ninja Foodi Digital Air Fry Oven" and turn the dial to select *Air Fry* mode. Press *Time/Slice* button and again turn the dial to set the cooking time to 12 minutes.
- Now, push *Temp/Darkness* button and rotate the dial to set the temperature at 350 Degrees °F or (176 Degrees °C).
- Press *Start/Pause* button to start your Air Fry Oven. When the unit beeps to show that it is preheated, open the oven door and grease the air fry basket.
- Place the chicken breasts into the prepared air fry basket and insert in the oven. Flip the chicken breasts once halfway through. When cooking time is completed, open the oven door and serve hot with mashed potatoes.

Nutrition Values Per Serving: Calories: 556; Fat: 22.2g; Sat Fat: 5.3g; Carbs: 25.1g; Fiber: 4.8g; Sugar: 1.4g; Protein: 61.6g

Buttered Turkey Breast

Ingredients for Serving: 10

1 (6-pound) boneless turkey breast.

5 carrots, peeled and cut into chunks

1 cup chicken broth.

¼ cup butter

Salt and ground black pepper, to taste.

Directions and Ready in About: 1 hr. 30-Minutes.

- Take a pan, heat the oil over medium heat and the carrots for about 4-5 minutes. Add the turkey breast and cook for about 10 minutes or until golden brown from both sides. Remove from the heat and stir in salt, black pepper and broth. Transfer the mixture into a baking dish.
- Press *Power* button of "Ninja Foodi Digital Air Fry Oven" and turn the dial to select *Bake* mode. Press *Time/Slice* button and again turn the dial to set the cooking time to 60 minutes.
- Now, push *Temp/Darkness* button and rotate the dial to set the temperature at 375 Degrees °F or (190 Degrees °C). Press *Start/Pause* button to start your Air Fry Oven. When the unit beeps to show that it is preheated, open the oven door.
- Arrange the baking dish over the wire rack and insert in the oven. Once the cooking time is completed, open the oven door and with tongs, place the turkey onto a cutting board for about 5 minutes before slicing.
- Cut into desired-sized slices and serve alongside carrots or with fresh salad.

Nutrition Values Per Serving: Calories: 322; Fat: 6g; Sat Fat: 3g; Carbs: 3.1g; Fiber: 0.8g; Sugar: 1.6g; Protein: 6.2g

Herbed Whole Chicken

Ingredients for Serving: 8

1 (4½-pound) whole chicken, necks and giblets removed.

3 tbsp. olive oil, divided.

1 tbsp. fresh basil, chopped.

1 tbsp. fresh oregano, chopped.

1 tbsp. fresh thyme, chopped.

Salt and ground black pepper, to taste.

Directions and Ready in About: 1 hr. 15-Minutes.

- Take a bowl, mix together the herbs, salt and black pepper. Coat the chicken with 2 tbsp. of oil and then, rub inside, outside and underneath the skin with half of the herb mixture generously.
- Press *Power* button of "Ninja Foodi Digital Air Fry Oven" and turn the dial to select *Air Fry* mode. Press *Time/Slice* button and again turn the dial to set the cooking time to 60 minutes.
- Now, push *Temp/Darkness* button and rotate the dial to set the temperature at 360 Degrees °F or (182 Degrees °C).
- Press *Start/Pause* button to start your Air Fry Oven. When the unit beeps to show that it is preheated, open the oven door.
- Arrange the chicken into the greased air fry basket, breast-side down and insert in the oven. After 30 minutes of cooking, arrange the chicken, breast-side up and coat with the remaining oil.
- Then rub with the remaining herb mixture. Once the cooking time is completed, open the oven door and place the chicken onto a cutting board for about 10 minutes before carving.
- With a sharp knife, cut the chicken into desired sized pieces and serve with roasted vegetables.

Nutrition Values Per Serving: Calories: 533; Fat: 24.3g; Sat Fat: 6g; Carbs: 0.6g; Fiber: 0.4g; Sugar: 0g; Protein: 73.9g

Spiced Turkey Breast

Ingredients for Serving: 8

1 (3-pound) turkey breast

2 tbsp. fresh rosemary, chopped.

1 tsp. smoked paprika

1 tsp. cayenne pepper.

1 tsp. ground cumin

1 tsp. ground cinnamon

Salt and ground black pepper, to taste.

Directions and Ready in About: 55-Minutes.

- Take a bowl, mix together the rosemary, spices, salt and black pepper. Rub the turkey breast with rosemary mixture evenly. With kitchen twines, tie the turkey breast to keep it compact.
- Press *Power* button of "Ninja Foodi Digital Air Fry Oven" and turn the dial to select *Air Fry* mode. Press *Time/Slice* button and again turn the dial to set the cooking time to 45 minutes.

- Now, push *Temp/Darkness* button and rotate the dial to set the temperature at 360 Degrees °F or (182 Degrees °C).
- Press *Start/Pause* button to start your Air Fry Oven. When the unit beeps to show that it is preheated, open the oven door.
- Arrange the turkey breast into the greased air fry basket and insert in oven. Once the cooking time is completed, open the oven door and place the turkey breast onto a platter for about 5-10 minutes before slicing.
- With a sharp knife, cut the turkey breast into desired sized slices and serve alongside with the cranberry sauce.

Nutrition Values Per Serving: Calories: 190; Fat: 0.9g; Sat Fat: 0.1g; Carbs: 0.9g; Fiber: 0.5g; Sugar: 6g; Protein: 29.5g

Crispy Chicken Cutlets

Ingredients for Serving: 4

4 (6-ounce) (¼-inch thick) skinless, boneless chicken cutlets.

1½ cups breadcrumbs

¼ cup Parmesan cheese, grated.

2 large eggs

¾ cup flour

1 tbsp. mustard powder

Salt and ground black pepper, to taste.

Directions and Ready in About: 45-Minutes.

- Take a shallow bowl, add the flour. In a second bowl, crack the eggs and beat well. In a third bowl, mix together the breadcrumbs, cheese, mustard powder, salt and black pepper.
- Season the chicken with salt and black pepper. Coat the chicken with flour, then dip into beaten eggs and finally coat with the breadcrumbs mixture.
- Press *Power* button of "Ninja Foodi Digital Air Fry Oven" and turn the dial to select *Air Fry* mode. Press *Time/Slice* button and again turn the dial to set the cooking time to 30 minutes.
- Now, push *Temp/Darkness* button and rotate the dial to set the temperature at 355 Degrees °F or (179 Degrees °C). Press *Start/Pause* button to start your Air Fry Oven. When the unit beeps to show that it is preheated, open the oven door and grease the air fry basket.
- Place the chicken cutlets into the prepared air fry basket and insert in the oven. When cooking time is completed, open the oven door and serve hot with favorite greens.

Nutrition Values Per Serving: Calories: 526; Fat: 13g; Sat Fat: 4.2g; Carbs: 48.6g; Fiber: 3g; Sugar: 3g; Protein: 51.7g

Roasted Goose

Ingredients for Serving: 12

8 lbs. goose

½ yellow onion, peeled and chopped.

1 head garlic, peeled and chopped.

½ cup wine

1 tsp. dried thyme.

Juice of a lemon

Salt and pepper

Directions and Ready in About: 55-Minutes.

- Place the goose in a sheet pan and whisk the rest of the ingredients in a bowl. Pour this thick sauce over the goose and brush it liberally.
- Transfer the goose to the "Ninja Foodi Digital Air Fry Oven" and close the door. Select "Air Roast" mode by rotating the dial.
- Press the *Temp/Darkness* button and change the value to 355 Degrees °F or (179 Degrees °C). Press the *Time/Slice* button and change the value to 40 minutes, then press *Start/Pause* to begin cooking. Serve warm with cucumber salad and toasted bread slices.

Nutrition Values Per Serving: Calories: 449; Fat: 13g; Sodium: 432mg; Carbs: 31g; Fiber: 3g; Sugar: 1g; Protein: 23g

Herbed Turkey Legs

Ingredients for Serving: 2

2 garlic cloves, minced.	¼ tsp. dried oregano.
2 turkey legs	¼ tsp. dried rosemary
1 tbsp. butter, melted.	Salt and ground black pepper, to taste.
¼ tsp. dried thyme	

Directions and Ready in About: 45-Minutes.

- Take a large bowl, mix together the butter, garlic, herbs, salt and black pepper. Add the turkey legs and coat with mixture generously.
- Press *Power* button of "Ninja Foodi Digital Air Fry Oven" and turn the dial to select *Air Fry* mode. Press *Time/Slice* button and again turn the dial to set the cooking time to 27 minutes.
- Now, push *Temp/Darkness* button and rotate the dial to set the temperature at 350 Degrees °F or (176 Degrees °C).
- Press *Start/Pause* button to start your Air Fry Oven. When the unit beeps to show that it is preheated, open the oven door.
- Arrange the turkey wings into the greased air fry basket and insert in the oven. Once the cooking time is completed, open the oven door and serve hot with cabbage slaw.

Nutrition Values Per Serving: Calories: 592; Fat: 22g; Sat Fat: 8.7g; Carbs: 1.3g; Fiber: 0.3g; Sugar: 0g; Protein: 91.6g

Marinated Spicy Chicken Legs

Ingredients for Serving: 4

4 chicken legs	1 tsp. ground turmeric
4 tbsp. plain yogurt.	2 tsp. red chili powder.
3 tbsp. fresh lemon juice	1 tsp. ground cumin
3 tsp. ginger paste	Salt, to taste.
3 tsp. garlic paste.	Ground black pepper, to taste.
1 tsp. ground coriander	

Directions and Ready in About: 30-Minutes.

- Take a bowl, mix together the chicken legs, lemon juice, ginger, garlic and salt. Set aside for about 15 minutes. Meanwhile, in another bowl, mix together the yogurt and spices.

- Add the chicken legs and coat with the spice mixture generously. Cover the bowl and refrigerate for at least 10-12 hours.
- Press *Power* button of "Ninja Foodi Digital Air Fry Oven" and turn the dial to select *Air Fry* mode. Press *Time/Slice* button and again turn the dial to set the cooking time to 20 minutes.
- Now, push *Temp/Darkness* button and rotate the dial to set the temperature at 440 Degrees °F or (227 Degrees °C). Press *Start/Pause* button to start your Air Fry Oven. When the unit beeps to show that it is preheated, open the oven door and grease the air fry basket.
- Place the chicken legs into the prepared air fry basket and insert in the oven. When cooking time is completed, open the oven door and serve hot with fresh greens.

Nutrition Values Per Serving: Calories: 461| Fat: 17.6g; Sat Fat: 5g; Carbs: 4.3g; Fiber: 0.9g; Sugar: 1.5g; Protein: 67.1g

Spiced Orange Duck

Ingredients for Serving: 8

1 (5- to 6-pound) duck, skinned.	2 parsley sprigs
1 juice orange, halved	½ carrot
4 fresh thyme sprigs.	½ celery rib
4 fresh marjoram sprigs	1 tbsp. salt
1 small onion, cut into wedges	1 tsp. ground coriander.
½ cup dry white wine.	½ tsp. ground cumin
½ cup chicken broth	1 tsp. black pepper.

Directions and Ready in About: 1 hr. 15-Minutes.

- Place the Pekin duck in a sheet pan and whisk orange juice and the rest of the ingredients in a bowl. Pour the herb sauce over the duck and brush it liberally. Transfer the duck to the "Ninja Foodi Digital Air Fry Oven" and close the door. Select *Air Fry* mode by rotating the dial.
- Press the *Time/Slice* button and change the value to 60 minutes. Press the *Temp/Darkness* button and change the value to 350 Degrees °F or (176 Degrees °C). Press *Start/Pause* to begin cooking. Continue basting the duck during baking. Serve warm with chili garlic sauce.

Nutrition Values Per Serving: Calories: 531; Fat: 20g; Carbs: 30g; Fiber: 0.9g; Sugar: 1.4g; Protein: 24.6g

Blackened Chicken Bake

Ingredients for Serving: 4

4 chicken breasts.	Chopped parsley, for garnish.
2 tsp. olive oil	

Seasoning:

1 ½ tbsp. brown sugar.	½ tsp. salt and pepper
¼ tsp. garlic powder	1 tsp. paprika
1 tsp. dried oregano.	

Directions and Ready in About: 33-Minutes.

- Mix olive oil with brown sugar, paprika, oregano, garlic powder, salt and black pepper in a bowl. Place the chicken breasts in the baking tray of the "Ninja Foodi Digital Air Fry Oven".
- Transfer the tray to the "Ninja Foodi Digital Air Fry Oven" and close the door. Select *Bake* mode by rotating the dial.
- Press the *Time/Slice* button and change the value to 18 minutes. Press the *Temp/Darkness* button and change the value to 425 Degrees °F or (218 Degrees °C).
- Press *Start/Pause* to begin cooking. Serve warm with roasted veggies.

Nutrition Values Per Serving: Calories: 419; Fat: 14g; Sodium: 442mg; Carbs: 23g; Fiber: 0.4g; Sugar: 2g; Protein: 32.3g

Parmesan Chicken Meatballs

Ingredients for Serving: 4

1 lb. ground chicken	1 large egg, beaten
½ cup Parmesan cheese, grated.	1 tsp. garlic powder.
½ cup ground pork rinds, for crust	1 tsp. paprika
	1 tsp. kosher salt
½ cup pork rinds, ground.	½ tsp. pepper.

Directions and Ready in About: 27-Minutes.

- Toss all the meatball ingredients in a bowl and mix well. Make small meatballs out of this mixture and roll them in the pork rinds.
- Place the coated meatballs in the air fry basket. Transfer the basket to the "Ninja Foodi Digital Air Fry Oven" and close the door.
- Select *Bake* mode by rotating the dial. Press the *Time/Slice* button and change the value to 12 minutes.
- Press the *Temp/Darkness* button and change the value to 400 Degrees °F or (204 Degrees °C). Press *Start/Pause* to begin cooking. Once preheated, place the air fry basket inside and close its oven door. Serve warm with fresh herbs on top and a bowl of steamed rice.

Nutrition Values Per Serving: Calories: 486; Fat: 13g; Sodium: 611mg; Carbs: 15g; Fiber: 0g; Sugar: g4; Protein: 26g

Chicken and Rice Casserole

Ingredients for Serving: 4

2 lbs. bone-in chicken thighs.	2 large onions, chopped.
2 large red bell peppers, chopped.	2 tbsp. tomato paste
2 cups chicken broth	2 tbsp. parsley, chopped.
3 cups brown rice, thawed.	6 tbsp. sour cream
5 cloves garlic, chopped.	1 tsp. olive oil
1 tbsp. sweet Hungarian paprika	1 tsp. hot Hungarian paprika.
	Salt and black pepper

Directions and Ready in About: 38-Minutes.

- Season the chicken with salt, black pepper and olive oil. Sear the chicken in a skillet for 5 minutes per side, then transfer to a casserole dish.
- Sauté onion in the same skillet until soft. Toss in garlic, peppers and paprika, then sauté for 3 minutes. Stir in tomato paste, chicken broth and rice.
- Mix well and cook until rice is soft, then add sour cream and parsley. Spread the mixture over the chicken in the casserole dish.
- Transfer the dish to the "Ninja Foodi Digital Air Fry Oven" and close the door. Transfer the sandwich to the "Ninja Foodi Digital Air Fry Oven" and close the door.
- Select *Bake* mode by rotating the dial. Press the *Time/Slice* button and change the value to 10 minutes.
- Press the *Temp/Darkness* button and change the value to 375 Degrees °F or (190 Degrees °C). Press *Start/Pause* to begin cooking. Serve warm casserole with toasted bread slices.

Nutrition Values Per Serving: Calories: 454; Fat: 25g; Sodium: 412mg; Carbs: 22g; Fiber: 0.2g; Sugar: 1g; Protein: 28.3g

Spanish Style Chicken Bake

Ingredients for Serving: 4

½ lb. potatoes, quartered	½ red onion, quartered.
4 tomatoes, quartered.	4 garlic cloves
⅛ cup chorizo	¼ tsp. paprika powder
½ green bell pepper, julienned	¼ tsp. dried oregano
4 chicken thighs, boneless.	Salt, to taste.
½ onion, quartered	Black pepper, to taste.

Directions and Ready in About: 40-Minutes.

- Toss chicken, veggies and all the ingredients in a baking tray. Transfer the tray to the "Ninja Foodi Digital Air Fry Oven" and close the door.
- Select *Bake* mode by rotating the dial. Press the *Time/Slice* button and change the value to 25 minutes.
- Press the *Temp/Darkness* button and change the value to 425 Degrees °F or (218 Degrees °C). Press *Start/Pause* to begin cooking. Serve warm with warmed pita bread.

Nutrition Values Per Serving: Calories: 478; Fat: 8g; Sodium: 339mg; Carbs: 28g; Fiber: 1g; Sugar: 2g; Protein: 33g

Easy Turkey Breast

Ingredients for Serving: 6

1 (2¾-pound) bone-in, skin-on turkey breast half	Salt and ground black pepper, to taste.

Directions and Ready in About: 1 hr. 30-Minutes.

- Rub the turkey breast with the salt and black pepper evenly. Arrange the turkey breast into a greased baking pan.
- Press *Power* button of "Ninja Foodi Digital Air Fry Oven" and turn the dial to select *Bake* mode. Press

- *Time/Slice* button and again turn the dial to set the cooking time to 1 hour 20 minutes.
- Now, push *Temp/Darkness* button and rotate the dial to set the temperature at 450 Degrees °F or (232 Degrees °C). Press *Start/Pause* button to start your Air Fry Oven. When the unit beeps to show that it is preheated, open the oven door.
- Arrange the pan over the wire rack and insert in the oven. When cooking time is completed, open the oven door and place the turkey breast onto a cutting board.
- With a piece of foil, cover the turkey breast for about 20 minutes before slicing. With a sharp knife, cut the turkey breast into desired size slices and serve with alongside the steamed veggies.

Nutrition Values Per Serving: Calories: 221; Fat: 0.8g; Sat Fat: 0g; Carbs: 0g; Fiber: 0g; Sugar: 0g; Protein: 51.6g

Roasted Duck

Ingredients for Serving: 6

6 lbs. whole Pekin duck.	1 lemon, chopped.
5 garlic cloves, chopped.	Salt, to taste.

For the Glaze:

1 lemon, juiced.	½ cup balsamic vinegar.
¼ cup honey	

Directions and Ready in About: 3 hr.s 15 Minutes

- Place the Pekin duck in a baking tray and add garlic, lemon and salt on top. Whisk honey, the juiced lemon and vinegar in a bowl. Brush this glaze over the duck liberally. Marinate overnight in the refrigerator.
- Remove the duck from the marinade and move the duck to sheet pan. Transfer the sheet pan to the "Ninja Foodi Digital Air Fry Oven" and close the door.
- Select "Air Roast" mode by rotating the dial. Press the *Time/Slice* button and change the value to 2 hours.
- Press the *Temp/Darkness* button and change the value to 350 Degrees °F or (176 Degrees °C). Press *Start/Pause* to begin cooking.
- When cooking completed, set the oven the temperature to 350 Degrees °F or (176 Degrees °C) and time to 1 hour at Air Roast mode. Press *Start/Pause* to begin. When it is cooked, serve warm with roasted green beans and mashed potatoes.

Nutrition Values Per Serving: Calories: 465; Fat: 5g; Sodium: 422mg; Carbs: 16g; Fiber: 0g; Sugar: 1g; Protein: 25g

Chicken Kebabs

Ingredients for Serving: 6

16 oz. skinless chicken breasts, cubed.	½ yellow pepper sliced.
½ zucchini sliced	¼ red onion sliced
½ green pepper sliced.	4 cherry tomatoes.
½ red pepper sliced	1 tbsp. chicken seasoning

2 tbsp. soy sauce.	salt and pepper to taste
1 tsp. BBQ seasoning	cooking spray.

Directions and Ready in About: 35-Minutes.

- Toss chicken and veggies with all the spices and seasoning in a bowl. Alternatively, thread them on skewers and place these skewers in the air fry basket.
- Transfer the basket to the "Ninja Foodi Digital Air Fry Oven" and close the door. Select *Air Fry* mode by rotating the dial.
- Press the *Time/Slice* button and change the value to 20 minutes. Press the *Temp/Darkness* button and change the value to 350 Degrees °F or (176 Degrees °C).
- Press *Start/Pause* to begin cooking. Flip the skewers when cooked halfway through, then resume cooking. Serve warm with roasted veggies on the side.

Nutrition Values Per Serving: Calories: 434; Fat: 16g; Sodium: 462mg; Carbs: 13g; Fiber: 0.4g; Sugar: 3g; Protein: 35.3g

Oven Baked Duck

Ingredients for Serving: 4

2 lbs. Piper potatoes.	4 cloves garlic, chopped.
1 ½ sprigs fresh rosemary	1 ½ red onions, chopped.
1 ½ carrot	½ nutmeg
2 cm piece fresh ginger.	Black pepper
1 ½ bay leaves	Juice from 1 orange
4 cups chicken stock	a few stalks celery
1 whole duck	

Directions and Ready in About: 2 hr.s 35-Minutes.

- Place duck in a large cooking pot and add broth along with all the ingredients. Cook this duck for 2 hours on a simmer, then transfer to the sheet pan.
- Transfer the sheet pan to the "Ninja Foodi Digital Air Fry Oven" and close the door. Select *Air Fry* mode by rotating the dial.
- Press the *Time/Slice* button and change the value to 20 minutes. Press the *Temp/Darkness* button and change the value to 350 Degrees °F or (176 Degrees °C). Press *Start/Pause* to begin cooking. Serve warm with a fresh crouton salad.

Nutrition Values Per Serving: Calories: 505; Fat: 7.9g; Carbs: 21.8g; Fiber: 2.6g; Sugar: 7g; Protein: 37.2g

Creamy Chicken Casserole

Ingredients for Serving: 4

Chicken Mushroom Casserole

2 ½ lbs. chicken breasts, cut into strips.	3 garlic cloves, minced.
1 lb. white mushrooms, sliced.	1 cup all-purpose flour
1 medium onion, diced	6 tbsp. olive oil
	1 ½ tsp. salt
	¼ tsp. black pepper.

For the Sauce:

1 cup half and half cream.	1 tbsp. lemon juice
½ cup milk, optional	3 tbsp. unsalted butter.
1 cups chicken broth, optional	3 tbsp. all-purpose flour

Directions and Ready in About: 1 hr. 2-Minutes.

- Butter a casserole dish and toss in chicken with mushrooms and all the casserole ingredients. Prepare the sauce in a suitable pan. Add butter and melt over moderate heat.
- Stir in all-purpose flour and whisk well for 2 minutes, then pour in milk, chicken broth, lemon juice and cream. Mix well and pour this creamy white sauce over the chicken mix in the casserole dish.
- Transfer the dish to the "Ninja Foodi Digital Air Fry Oven" and close the door. Select *Bake* mode by rotating the dial.
- Press the *Time/Slice* button and change the value to 45 minutes. Press the *Temp/Darkness* button and change the value to 350 Degrees °F or (176 Degrees °C). Press *Start/Pause* to begin cooking. Serve warm with steaming white rice.

Nutrition Values Per Serving: Calories: 601; Fat: 16g; Carbs: 32g; Fiber: 0.3g; Sugar: 0.1g; Protein: 28.2g

Chicken Kabobs

Ingredients for Serving: 2

1 (8-ounce) chicken breast, cut into medium-sized pieces.	½ tsp. lemon zest, grated.
	1 tsp. plain Greek yogurt
3 garlic cloves, grated.	1 tsp. olive oil
1 tbsp. fresh lemon juice.	Salt and ground black pepper, to taste.
1 tbsp. fresh oregano, minced.	

Directions and Ready in About: 24-Minutes.

- Take a large bowl, add the chicken, lemon juice, garlic, oregano, lemon zest, salt and black pepper and toss to coat well.
- Cover the bowl and refrigerate overnight. Remove the bowl from the refrigerator and stir in the yogurt and oil.
- Thread the chicken pieces onto the metal skewers. Press *Power* button of "Ninja Foodi Digital Air Fry Oven" and turn the dial to select *Air Fry* mode.
- Press *Time/Slice* button and again turn the dial to set the cooking time to 9 minutes. Now, push *Temp/Darkness* button and rotate the dial to set the temperature at 350 Degrees °F or (176 Degrees °C).
- Press *Start/Pause* button to start your Air Fry Oven. When the unit beeps to show that it is preheated, open the oven door and grease the air fry basket.
- Place the skewers into the prepared air fry basket and insert in the oven. Flip the skewers once halfway through. When cooking time is completed, open the oven door and serve hot with alongside fresh salad.

Nutrition Values Per Serving: Calories: 167; Fat: 5.5g; Sat Fat: 0.5g; Carbs: 3.4g; Fiber: 0.5g; Sugar: 1.1g; Protein: 24.8g

Cheesy Turkey Burgers

Ingredients for Serving: 2

8 oz. ground turkey breast.	2 tsp. fresh oregano, chopped.
¼ cup feta cheese, crumbled	½ tsp. red pepper flakes, crushed
2 garlic cloves, grated.	Salt, to taste.
1½ tbsp. extra-virgin olive oil	

Directions and Ready in About: 25-Minutes.

- Take a large bowl, add all the ingredients except for feta cheese and mix until well combined. Make 2 (½-inch-thick) patties from the mixture.
- Press *Power* button of "Ninja Foodi Digital Air Fry Oven" and turn the dial to select *Air Fry* mode. Press *Time/Slice* button and again turn the dial to set the cooking time to 15 minutes.
- Now, push *Temp/Darkness* button and rotate the dial to set the temperature at 360 Degrees °F or (182 Degrees °C).
- Press *Start/Pause* button to start your Air Fry Oven. When the unit beeps to show that it is preheated, open the oven door.
- Arrange the patties into the greased air fry basket and insert in the oven. Flip the turkey burgers once halfway through.
- Once the cooking time is completed, open the oven door and serve hot with the topping of feta cheese and with fresh greens.

Nutrition Values Per Serving: Calories: 364; Fat: 23.1g; Sat Fat: 6.7g; Carbs: 3g; Fiber: 0.8g; Sugar: 0.9g; Protein: 35.6g

Brine Soaked Turkey

Ingredients for Serving: 4

7 lbs. bone-in, skin-on turkey breast

Brine:

3 cloves garlic, smashed.	½ onion
5 sprigs fresh thyme	1 lemon
½ cup salt	black pepper.
3 bay leaves.	

Turkey Breast:

4 tbsp. butter, softened.	½ tsp. black pepper
¼ tsp. dried thyme	½ tsp. garlic powder.
¼ tsp. dried oregano.	

Directions and Ready in About: 1 hr. 15-Minutes.

- Mix the turkey brine ingredients in a pot and soak the turkey in the brine overnight. The next day, remove the soaked turkey from the brine.
- Whisk the butter, black pepper, garlic powder, oregano and thyme. Brush the butter mixture over the turkey, then place it in a sheet pan.

- Transfer the pan to the "Ninja Foodi Digital Air Fry Oven" and close the door.
- Select "Air Roast" mode by rotating the dial. Press the *Time/Slice* button and change the value to 60 minutes. Press the *Temp/Darkness* button and change the value to 375 Degrees °F or (190 Degrees °C).
- Press *Start/Pause* to begin cooking. Slice and serve warm with fresh cucumber and couscous salad.

Nutrition Values Per Serving: Calories: 553; Fat: 2.4g; Carbs: 18g; Fiber: 2.3g; Sugar: 1.2g; Protein: 23.2g

Herbed Cornish Game Hen

Ingredients for Serving: 4

2 Cornish game hens.

2 tbsp. avocado oil

½ tsp. dried thyme.

½ tsp. dried basil

½ tsp. dried oregano

½ tsp. dried rosemary.

Salt and ground black pepper, to taste.

Directions and Ready in About: 50-Minutes.

- Take a bowl, mix together the oil, dried herbs, salt and black pepper. Rub each hen with herb mixture evenly.
- Press *Power* button of "Ninja Foodi Digital Air Fry Oven" and turn the dial to select *Air Fry* mode. Press *Time/Slice* button and again turn the dial to set the cooking time to 35 minutes.
- Now, push *Temp/Darkness* button and rotate the dial to set the temperature at 360 Degrees °F or (182 Degrees °C).
- Press *Start/Pause* button to start your Air Fry Oven. When the unit beeps to show that it is preheated, open the oven door and grease the air fry basket.
- Arrange the hens into the prepared basket, breast side down and insert in the oven. When cooking time is completed, open the oven door and transfer the hens onto a platter. Cut each hen in pieces and serve alongside with roasted veggies.

Nutrition Values Per Serving: Calories: 895; Fat: 62.9g; Sat Fat: 17.4g; Carbs: 0.7g; Fiber: 0.5g; Sugar: 0g; Protein: 75.9g

Crispy Chicken Thighs

Ingredients for Serving: 4

4 (4-ounce) skin-on chicken thighs.

½ cup all-purpose flour.

1 egg

1½ tbsp. Cajun seasoning

1 tsp. seasoning salt.

Directions and Ready in About: 40-Minutes.

- Take a shallow bowl, mix together the flour, Cajun seasoning and salt. In another bowl, crack the egg and beat well.
- Coat each chicken thigh with the flour mixture, then dip into beaten egg and finally, coat with the flour mixture again.
- Shake off the excess flour thoroughly. Press *Power* button of "Ninja Foodi Digital Air Fry Oven" and turn the dial to select *Air Fry* mode. Press *Time/Slice* button and again turn the dial to set the cooking time to 25 minutes.

- Now, push *Temp/Darkness* button and rotate the dial to set the temperature at 390 Degrees °F or (199 Degrees °C).
- Press *Start/Pause* button to start your Air Fry Oven. When the unit beeps to show that it is preheated, open the oven door and grease the air fry basket.
- Place the chicken thighs into the prepared air fry basket and insert in the oven. When cooking time is completed, open the oven door and serve hot with ketchup.

Nutrition Values Per Serving: Calories: 288; Fat: 9.6g; Sat Fat: 2.7g; Carbs: 12g; Fiber: 0.4g; Sugar: 0.1g; Protein: 35.9g

Gingered Chicken Drumsticks

Ingredients for Serving: 3

3 (6-ounce) chicken drumsticks.

¼ cup full-fat coconut milk

2 tsp. ground turmeric.

2 tsp. fresh ginger, minced.

2 tsp. galangal, minced.

Salt, to taste.

Directions and Ready in About: 35-Minutes.

- Place the coconut milk, galangal, ginger and spices in a large bowl and mix well. Add the chicken drumsticks and coat with the marinade generously.
- Refrigerate to marinate for at least 6-8 hours. Press *Power* button of "Ninja Foodi Digital Air Fry Oven" and turn the dial to select *Air Fry* mode. Press *Time/Slice* button and again turn the dial to set the cooking time to 25 minutes.
- Now, push *Temp/Darkness* button and rotate the dial to set the temperature at 375 Degrees °F or (190 Degrees °C).
- Press *Start/Pause* button to start your Air Fry Oven. When the unit beeps to show that it is preheated, open the oven door and grease the air fry basket.
- Place the chicken drumsticks into the prepared air fry basket and insert in the oven. When cooking time is completed, open the oven door and serve hot alongside with the lemony couscous.

Nutrition Values Per Serving: Calories: 347; Fat: 14.8g; Sat Fat: 6.9g; Carbs: 3.8g; Fiber: 1.1g; Sugar: 0.8g; Protein: 47.6g

Potato Chicken Bake

Ingredients for Serving: 4

1.5 lbs. boneless skinless chicken

¾ cup mozzarella cheese, shredded.

1 tbsp. garlic, minced.

4 potatoes, diced

1.5 tbsp. olive oil

⅛ tsp. salt

⅛ tsp. pepper

Parsley, chopped.

Directions and Ready in About: 40-Minutes.

- Toss chicken and potatoes with all the spices and oil in a sheet pan. Drizzle the cheese on top of the chicken and potato.
- Transfer the pan to the "Ninja Foodi Digital Air Fry Oven" and close the door. Select *Bake* mode by rotating the

dial. Press the *Time/Slice* button and change the value to 25 minutes.

- Press the *Temp/Darkness* button and change the value to 375 Degrees °F or (190 Degrees °C). Press *Start/Pause* to begin cooking. Serve warm with avocado guacamole.

Nutrition Values Per Serving: Calories: 462; Fat: 14g; Sodium: 220mg; Carbs: 16g; Fiber: 0.2g; Sugar: 1g; Protein: 26g

Crispy Chicken Legs

Ingredients for Serving: 3

3 (8-ounce) chicken legs.	1 tsp. ground cumin.
2 cups white flour	1 tsp. garlic powder
1 cup buttermilk.	1 tsp. paprika
1 tbsp. olive oil	Salt and ground black pepper, to taste.
1 tsp. onion powder	

Directions and Ready in About: 35-Minutes.

- Take a bowl, place the chicken legs and buttermilk and refrigerate for about 2 hours.
- In a shallow dish, mix together the flour and spices. Remove the chicken from buttermilk. Coat the chicken legs with flour mixture, then dip into buttermilk and finally, coat with the flour mixture again.
- Press *Power* button of "Ninja Foodi Digital Air Fry Oven" and turn the dial to select *Air Fry* mode. Press *Time/Slice* button and again turn the dial to set the cooking time to 20 minutes.
- Now, push *Temp/Darkness* button and rotate the dial to set the temperature at 355 Degrees °F or (179 Degrees °C). Press *Start/Pause* button to start your Air Fry Oven. When the unit beeps to show that it is preheated, open the oven door and grease the air fry basket.
- Arrange chicken legs into the prepared air fry basket and drizzle with the oil. Insert the basket in the oven. When cooking time is completed, open the oven door and serve hot with your favorite dip.

Nutrition Values Per Serving: Calories: 817; Fat: 23.3g; Sat Fat: 5.9g; Carbs: 69.5g; Fiber: 2.7g; Sugar: 4.7g; Protein: 77.4g

Meat Recipes

Herbed Leg of Lamb

Ingredients for Serving: 6

2¼ lbs. boneless leg of lamb

2 fresh thyme sprigs

2 fresh rosemary sprigs

2 tbsp. olive oil

Salt and ground black pepper, to taste.

Directions and Ready in About: 1 hr. 25-Minutes.

- Coat the leg of lamb with oil and sprinkle with salt and black pepper. Wrap the leg of lamb with herb sprigs.
- Press *Power* button of "Ninja Foodi Digital Air Fry Oven" and turn the dial to select *Air Fry* mode. Press *Time/Slice* button and again turn the dial to set the cooking time to 75 minutes.
- Now, push *Temp/Darkness* button and rotate the dial to set the temperature at 300 Degrees °F or (149 Degrees °C).
- Press *Start/Pause* button to start your Air Fry Oven. When the unit beeps to show that it is preheated, open the oven door.
- Arrange the leg of lamb into the greased air fry basket and insert in the oven. Immediately set the temperature at 355 Degrees °F or (179 Degrees °C).
- Once the cooking time is completed, open the oven door and place the leg of lamb onto a cutting board for about 10 minutes. Cut the leg of lamb into desired-sized pieces and serve alongside with the roasted Brussels sprout.

Nutrition Values Per Serving: Calories: 360; Fat: 17.3g; Sat Fat: 5.2g; Carbs: 0.7g; Fiber: 0.5g; Sugar: 0g; Protein: 47.8g

Glazed Beef Short Ribs

Ingredients for Serving: 4

2 lbs. bone-in beef short ribs.

¼ cup balsamic vinegar

½ cup low-sodium soy sauce.

½ tbsp. fresh ginger, finely grated

3 tbsp. scallions, chopped.

1 tbsp. sugar

½ tbsp. Sriracha

½ tsp. ground black pepper.

Directions and Ready in About: 23-Minutes.

- In a resealable bag, place all the ingredients. Seal the bag and shake to coat well. Refrigerate overnight.
- Press *Power* button of "Ninja Foodi Digital Air Fry Oven" and turn the dial to select *Air Fry* mode. Press *Time/Slice* button and again turn the dial to set the cooking time to 8 minutes.
- Now, push *Temp/Darkness* button and rotate the dial to set the temperature at 380 Degrees °F or (193 Degrees °C).
- Press *Start/Pause* button to start your Air Fry Oven. When the unit beeps to show that it is preheated, open the oven door.

- Place the ribs into the greased air fry basket and insert in the oven. Flip the ribs once halfway through. Once the cooking time is completed, open the oven door and serve hot with cucumber salad.

Nutrition Values Per Serving: Calories: 496; Fat: 20.5g; Sat Fat: 7.8g; Carbs: 6.5g; Fiber: 0.3g; Sugar: 5.2g; Protein: 67.7g

Mustard Lamb Loin Chops

Ingredients for Serving: 2

4 (4-ounce) lamb loin chops.

½ tbsp. white wine vinegar

1 tbsp. Dijon mustard.

½ tsp. dried tarragon

1 tsp. olive oil

Salt and ground black pepper, to taste.

Directions and Ready in About: 25-Minutes.

- Take a large bowl, mix together the mustard, vinegar, oil, tarragon, salt and black pepper. Add the chops and coat with the mixture generously.
- Arrange the chops onto the greased sheet pan. Press *Power* button of "Ninja Foodi Digital Air Fry Oven" and turn the dial to select *Bake* mode.
- Press *Time/Slice* button and again turn the dial to set the cooking time to 15 minutes. Now, push *Temp/Darkness* button and rotate the dial to set the temperature at 390 Degrees °F or (199 Degrees °C).
- Press *Start/Pause* button to start your Air Fry Oven. When the unit beeps to show that it is preheated, open the oven door and insert the sheet pan in the oven.
- Once the cooking time is completed, open the oven door and serve hot alongside with the feta spinach.

Nutrition Values Per Serving: Calories: 44; Fat: 19.3g; Sat Fat: 6.3g; Carbs: 0.5g; Fiber: 0.3g; Sugar: 0.1g; Protein: 64.1g

Crispy Sirloin Steaks

Ingredients for Serving: 2

3 (6-ounce) sirloin steaks, pounded.

¾ cup breadcrumbs

2 eggs

½ cup flour.

Salt and ground black pepper, to taste.

Directions and Ready in About: 24-Minutes.

- Take a shallow bowl, place the flour, salt and black pepper and mix well. In a second shallow bowl, beat the eggs. In a third shallow bowl, place the breadcrumbs. Coat the steak with flour, then dip into eggs and finally coat with the panko mixture.
- Press *Power* button of "Ninja Foodi Digital Air Fry Oven" and turn the dial to select *Air Fry* mode. Press *Time/Slice* button and again turn the dial to set the cooking time to 14 minutes.
- Now, push *Temp/Darkness* button and rotate the dial to set the temperature at 360 Degrees °F or (182 Degrees °C). Press *Start/Pause* button to start your Air Fry Oven. When the unit beeps to show that it is preheated, open the oven door.
- Arrange the steaks into the greased air fry basket and insert in the oven. Once the cooking time is completed,

open the oven door and serve hot with your favorite dipping sauce.

Nutrition Values Per Serving: Calories: 540; Fat: 15.2g; Sat Fat: 5.3g; Carbs: 35.6g; Fiber: 1.8g; Sugar: 2g; Protein: 61g

Balsamic Beef Top Roast

Ingredients for Serving: 10

3 lbs. beef top roast.

1 tbsp. balsamic vinegar

1 tbsp. butter, melted.

½ tsp. smoked paprika

½ tsp. red pepper flakes, crushed.

½ tsp. ground cumin

Salt and ground black pepper, to taste.

Directions and Ready in About: 55-Minutes.

- Take a bowl, add butter, vinegar, spices, salt and black pepper and mix well. Coat the roast with spice mixture generously. With kitchen twines, tie the roast to keep it compact. Arrange the roast onto the greased sheet pan.
- Press *Power* button of "Ninja Foodi Digital Air Fry Oven" and turn the dial to select *Air Fry* mode. Press *Time/Slice* button and again turn the dial to set the cooking time to 45 minutes.
- Now, push *Temp/Darkness* button and rotate the dial to set the temperature at 360 Degrees °F or (182 Degrees °C).
- Press *Start/Pause* button to start your Air Fry Oven. When the unit beeps to show that it is preheated, open the oven door and insert the sheet pan in the oven.
- Once the cooking time is completed, open the oven door and place the roast onto a cutting board for about 10 minutes before slicing. With a sharp knife, cut the roast into desired sized slices and serve alongside with the buttered green beans.

Nutrition Values Per Serving: Calories: 305; Fat: 17.1g; Sat Fat: 6.1g; Carbs: 0.1g; Fiber: 0.1g; Sugar: 0g; Protein: 35.1g

Zucchini Beef Meatloaf

Ingredients for Serving: 4

2 lbs. ground beef

¾ cup Panko breadcrumbs.

⅓ cup beef broth

½ cup onion, chopped

1 cup zucchini, shredded.

3 garlic cloves minced

3 tbsp. Worcestershire sauce

2 eggs

3 tbsp. fresh parsley, chopped.

½ tsp. ground paprika

¼ tsp. ground black pepper.

Salt to taste

Directions and Ready in About: 55-Minutes.

- Thoroughly mix ground beef with egg, zucchini, onion, garlic, crumbs, parsley, Worcestershire sauce, broth and all the seasoning ingredients in a bowl. Grease a meatloaf pan with oil and spread the minced beef in the pan. Transfer the pan to the "Ninja Foodi Digital Air Fry Oven" and close the door.
- Select *Air Fry* mode by rotating the dial. Press the *Time/Slice* button and change the value to 40 minutes.

Press the *Temp/Darkness* button and change the value to 375 Degrees °F or (190 Degrees °C). Press *Start/Pause* to begin cooking. Slice and serve with toasted bread slices.

Nutrition Values Per Serving: Calories: 325; Fat: 16g; Sodium: 431mg; Carbs: 22g; Fiber: 1.2g; Sugar: 4g; Protein: 23g

Herbs Crumbed Rack of Lamb

Ingredients for Serving: 5

1¾ lbs. rack of lamb

1 garlic clove, chopped finely.

½ cup panko breadcrumbs

1 egg

1 tbsp. butter, melted

1 tbsp. fresh rosemary, minced.

1 tbsp. fresh thyme, minced.

Salt and ground black pepper, to taste.

Directions and Ready in About: 45-Minutes.

- Take a bowl, mix together the butter, garlic, salt and black pepper. Coat the rack of lamb evenly with garlic mixture. In a shallow dish, beat the egg. In another dish, mix together the breadcrumbs and herbs.
- Dip the rack of lamb in beaten egg and then coat with breadcrumbs mixture. Press *Power* button of "Ninja Foodi Digital Air Fry Oven" and turn the dial to select *Air Fry* mode. Press *Time/Slice* button and again turn the dial to set the cooking time to 25 minutes.
- Now, push *Temp/Darkness* button and rotate the dial to set the temperature at 250 Degrees °F or (121 Degrees °C). Press *Start/Pause* button to start your Air Fry Oven. When the unit beeps to show that it is preheated, open the oven door and grease the air fry basket.
- Place the rack of lamb into the prepared air fry basket and insert in the oven. After 25 minutes of cooking,
- When cooking time is completed, open the oven door and set the temperature at 390 Degrees °F or (199 Degrees °C) for 5 minutes.
- When cooking time is completed, open the oven door and place the rack of lamb onto a cutting board for about 5-10 minutes. With a sharp knife, cut the rack of lamb into individual chops and serve with a drizzling of lemon juice.

Nutrition Values Per Serving: Calories: 331; Fat: 17.2g; Sat Fat: 6.7g; Carbs: 2.6g; Fiber: 0.5g; Sugar: 0g; Protein: 32.7g

Beef Tenderloin

Ingredients for Serving: 10

1 (3½-pound) beef tenderloin, trimmed.

2 tbsp. olive oil

Salt and ground black pepper, to taste.

Directions and Ready in About: 1 hr.

- With kitchen twine, tie the tenderloin. Rub the tenderloin with oil and season with salt and black pepper. Place the tenderloin into the greased sheet pan.
- Press *Power* button of "Ninja Foodi Digital Air Fry Oven" and turn the dial to select the "Air Roast" mode.

Press *Time/Slice* button and again turn the dial to set the cooking time to 50 minutes.

- Now, push *Temp/Darkness* button and rotate the dial to set the temperature at 400 Degrees °F or (204 Degrees °C).
- Press *Start/Pause* button to start your Air Fry Oven. When the unit beeps to show that it is preheated, open the oven door and insert the sheet pan in the oven.
- When cooking time is completed, open the oven door and place the tenderloin onto a platter for about 10 minutes before slicing. With a sharp knife, cut the tenderloin into desired sized slices and serve with lemony herbed couscous.

Nutrition Values Per Serving: Calories: 351; Fat: 17.3g; Sat Fat: 5.9g; Carbs: 0g; Fiber: 0g; Sugar: 0g; Protein: .46g

Pork Chops with Cashew Sauce

Ingredients for Serving: 8

1 small onion, peeled and chopped.

Salt and black pepper, to taste.

8 pork loin chops

For the Sauce:

1 oz. wheat flour.

1 cup cashew butter

6 fl. oz. milk

2 tbsp. coconut cream, whipping

6 fl. oz. beef stock

¼ cup cashews, chopped finely.

Salt and black pepper, to taste.

Directions and Ready in About: 1 hr. 7-Minutes.

- Place the pork loin chops and onion in a baking tray, then drizzle salt and black pepper on top. Transfer the tray to the "Ninja Foodi Digital Air Fry Oven" and close the door. Select *Bake* mode by rotating the dial. Press the *Time/Slice* button and change the value to 45 minutes.
- Press the *Temp/Darkness* button and change the value to 375 Degrees °F or (190 Degrees °C).
- Press *Start/Pause* to begin cooking. Prepare the white sauce by first melting butter in a suitable saucepan, then stir in cashews.
- Sauté for 5 minutes, then stir flour and stir cook for 2 minutes. Stir in the rest of the sauce ingredients and mix well. Pour the sauce over baked chops and serve with sautéed vegetables and toasted bread slices.

Nutrition Values Per Serving: Calories: 309; Fat: 25g; Sodium: 463mg; Carbs: 9g; Fiber: 0.3g; Sugar: 0.3g; Protein: 18g

Spiced Pork Shoulder

Ingredients for Serving: 4

2 lbs. skin-on pork shoulder.

1 tsp. ground cumin

½ tsp. garlic powder

1 tsp. cayenne pepper

½ tsp. onion powder.

Salt and ground black pepper, to taste.

Directions and Ready in About: 1 hr. 10-Minutes.

- Take a small bowl, place the spices, salt and black pepper and mix well. Arrange the pork shoulder onto a cutting board, skin-side down.
- Season the inner side of pork shoulder with salt and black pepper. With kitchen twines, tie the pork shoulder into a long round cylinder shape.
- Season the outer side of pork shoulder with spice mixture. Press *Power* button of "Ninja Foodi Digital Air Fry Oven" and turn the dial to select the "Air Roast" mode. Press *Time/Slice* button and again turn the dial to set the cooking time to 55 minutes.
- Now, push *Temp/Darkness* button and rotate the dial to set the temperature at 350 Degrees °F or (176 Degrees °C). Press *Start/Pause* button to start your Air Fry Oven.
- When the unit beeps to show that it is preheated, open the oven door and grease the air fry basket. Arrange the pork shoulder into air fry basket and insert in the oven.
- When cooking time is completed, open the oven door and place the pork shoulder onto a platter for about 10 minutes before slicing. With a sharp knife, cut the pork shoulder into desired sized slices and serve with southern-style grits.

Nutrition Values Per Serving: Calories: 445; Fat: 32.5g; Sat Fat: 11.9g; Carbs: 0.7g; Fiber: 0.2g; Sugar: 0.2g; Protein: 35.4g

Breaded Pork Chops

Ingredients for Serving: 3

4 oz. seasoned breadcrumbs.

1 tbsp. canola oil

1 egg

3 (6-ounce) pork chops

¼ cup plain flour.

Salt and ground black pepper, to taste.

Directions and Ready in About: 30-Minutes.

- Season each pork chop with salt and black pepper. Take a shallow bowl, place the flour. In a second bowl, crack the egg and beat well.
- In a third bowl, add the breadcrumbs and oil and mix until a crumbly mixture forms. Coat the pork chop with flour, then dip into beaten egg and finally, coat with the breadcrumbs mixture.
- Press *Power* button of "Ninja Foodi Digital Air Fry Oven" and turn the dial to select *Air Fry* mode. Press *Time/Slice* button and again turn the dial to set the cooking time to 15 minutes.
- Now, push *Temp/Darkness* button and rotate the dial to set the temperature at 400 Degrees °F or (204 Degrees °C). Press *Start/Pause* button to start your Air Fry Oven. When the unit beeps to show that it is preheated, open the oven door and grease the air fry basket.
- Place the lamb chops into the prepared air fry basket and insert in the oven. Flip the chops once halfway through. When cooking time is completed, open the oven door and serve hot with your favorite dipping sauce.

Nutrition Values Per Serving: Calories: 413; Fat: 20.2g; Sat Fat: 4.4g; Carbs: 31g; Fiber: 1.6g; Sugar: 0.1g; Protein: 28.3g

Lamb Rack with Lemon Crust

Ingredients for Serving: 3

¼ lb. dry breadcrumbs.

1 ⅔ lbs. frenched rack of lamb

1 egg, beaten

1 tsp. garlic, grated.

½ tsp. salt

1 tsp. cumin seeds.

1 tsp. ground cumin

1 tsp. oil

½ tsp. grated lemon rind

Salt and black pepper, to taste.

Directions and Ready in About: 40-Minutes.

- Place the lamb rack in a sheet pan and pour the whisked egg on top. Whisk the rest of the crusting ingredients in a bowl and spread over the lamb. Transfer the sheet pan to the "Ninja Foodi Digital Air Fry Oven" and close the door.
- Select *Air Fry* mode by rotating the dial. Press the *Time/Slice* button and change the value to 25 minutes. Press the *Temp/Darkness* button and change the value to 350 Degrees °F or (176 Degrees °C). Press *Start/Pause* to begin cooking. Serve warm with sautéed green beans and mashed potatoes.

Nutrition Values Per Serving: Calories: 455; Fat: 9.5g; Carbs: 13.4g; Fiber: 0.4g; Sugar: 0.4g; Protein: 28.3g

Herbed Lamb Loin Chops

Ingredients for Serving: 2.

4 (4-ounce) (½-inch thick) lamb loin chops

1 tsp. fresh thyme, minced.

1 tsp. fresh rosemary, minced.

2 garlic cloves, crushed

1 tsp. fresh oregano, minced.

Salt and ground black pepper, to taste.

Directions and Ready in About: 22-Minutes.

- Take a large bowl, place all ingredients and mix well. Refrigerate to marinate overnight. Arrange the chops onto the greased sheet pan.
- Press *Power* button of "Ninja Foodi Digital Air Fry Oven" and turn the dial to select *Bake* mode. Press *Time/Slice* button and again turn the dial to set the cooking time to 12 minutes.
- Now, push *Temp/Darkness* button and rotate the dial to set the temperature at 400 Degrees °F or (204 Degrees °C).
- Press *Start/Pause* button to start your Air Fry Oven. When the unit beeps to show that it is preheated, open the oven door and insert the sheet pan in the oven.
- Flip the chops once halfway through. Once the cooking time is completed, open the oven door and serve hot with steamed cauliflower.

Nutrition Values Per Serving: Calories: 432; Fat: 16.9g; Sat Fat: 6g; Carbs: 2.2g; Fiber: 0.8g; Sugar: 0.1g; Protein: 64g

Fried BBQ Pork Chops

Ingredients for Serving: 6

6 (8-ounce) pork loin chops.

½ cup BBQ sauce

Salt and ground black pepper, to taste.

Directions and Ready in About: 26-Minutes.

- With a meat tenderizer, tenderize the chops completely. Sprinkle the chops with a little salt and black pepper. Take a large bowl, add the BBQ sauce and chops and mix well. Refrigerate, covered for about 6-8 hours.
- Press *Power* button of "Ninja Foodi Digital Air Fry Oven" and turn the dial to select *Air Fry* mode. Press *Time/Slice* button and again turn the dial to set the cooking time to 16 minutes.
- Now, push *Temp/Darkness* button and rotate the dial to set the temperature at 355 Degrees °F or (179 Degrees °C). Press *Start/Pause* button to start your Air Fry Oven.
- When the unit beeps to show that it is preheated, open the oven door. Arrange the pork chops into the greased air fry basket and insert in the oven.
- Flip the chops once halfway through. Once the cooking time is completed, open the oven door and serve hot with roasted veggies.

Nutrition Values Per Serving: Calories: 757; Fat: 56.4g; Sat Fat: 21.1g; Carbs: 7.6g; Fiber: 0.1g; Sugar: 5.4g; Protein: 51g

Tarragon Beef Shanks

Ingredients for Serving: 4

2 lbs. beef shank

1 onion, diced.

2 stalks celery, diced

1 cup Marsala wine.

2 tbsp. olive oil

2 tbsp. dried tarragon

Salt and black pepper to taste.

Directions and Ready in About: 30-Minutes.

- Place the beef shanks in a baking pan. Whisk the rest of the ingredients in a bowl and pour over the shanks. Place these shanks in the air fry basket. Transfer the basket to the "Ninja Foodi Digital Air Fry Oven" and close the door.
- Select *Air Fry* mode by rotating the dial. Press the *Time/Slice* button and change the value to 15 minutes. Press the *Temp/Darkness* button and change the value to 375 Degrees °F or (190 Degrees °C). Press *Start/Pause* to begin cooking. Serve warm with sweet potato casserole.

Nutrition Values Per Serving: Calories: 425; Fat: 15g; Carbs: 12.3g; Fiber: 1.4g; Sugar: 3g; Protein: 23.3g

Lamb Kebabs

Ingredients for Serving: 4

2 oz. onion, chopped.

18 oz. lamb mince

1 tsp. chili powder.

1 tsp. cumin powder

1 egg

2 tsp. sesame oil

Directions and Ready in About: 35-Minutes.

- Whisk onion with egg, chili powder, oil, cumin powder and salt in a bowl. Add lamb to coat well, then thread it on the skewers. Place these lamb skewers in the air fry basket. Transfer the basket to the "Ninja Foodi Digital Air Fry Oven" and close the door. Select *Air Fry* mode by rotating the dial.
- Press the *Time/Slice* button and change the value to 20 minutes. Press the *Temp/Darkness* button and change the value to 395 Degrees °F or (202 Degrees °C). Press *Start/Pause* to begin cooking. Serve warm with garlic bread slices and fresh herbs on top.

Nutrition Values Per Serving: Calories: 405; Fat: 22.7g; Carbs: 6.1g; Fiber: 1.4g; Sugar: 0.9g; Protein: 45.2g

Seasoned Sirloin Steak

Ingredients for Serving: 2

2 (7-ounce) top sirloin steaks.

1 tbsp. steak seasoning

Salt and ground black pepper, to taste.

Directions and Ready in About: 22-Minutes.

- Season each steak with steak seasoning, salt and black pepper. Arrange the steaks onto the greased sheet pan.
- Press *Power* button of "Ninja Foodi Digital Air Fry Oven" and turn the dial to select *Air Fry* mode. Press *Time/Slice* button and again turn the dial to set the cooking time to 12 minutes.
- Now, push *Temp/Darkness* button and rotate the dial to set the temperature at 400 Degrees °F or (204 Degrees °C). Press *Start/Pause* button to start your Air Fry Oven.
- When the unit beeps to show that it is preheated, open the oven door and insert the sheet pan in the oven.
- Flip the steaks once halfway through. When cooking time is completed, open the oven door and serve hot with cheesy scalloped potatoes.

Nutrition Values Per Serving: Calories: 369; Fat: 12.4g; Sat Fat: 4.7g; Carbs: 0g; Fiber: 0g; Sugar: 0g; Protein: 60.2g

Orange Pork Chops

Ingredients for Serving: 6

8 garlic cloves, minced.

1 cup fresh cilantro, chopped finely.

½ cup olive oil

¼ cup fresh mint leaves, chopped finely.

6 thick-cut pork chops

3 tbsp. fresh orange juice

1 tsp. fresh orange zest, grated.

3 tbsp. fresh lime juice.

1 tsp. fresh lime zest, grated.

1 tsp. dried oregano, crushed

1 tsp. ground cumin

Salt and ground black pepper, to taste.

Directions and Ready in About: 30-Minutes.

- Take a bowl, place the oil, orange zest, orange juice, lime zest, lime juice, garlic, fresh herbs, oregano, cumin, salt and black pepper and beat until well combined.

- Take a small bowl, reserve ¼ cup of the marinade. In a large zip lock bag, place the remaining marinade and pork chops.
- Seal the bag and shake to coat well. Refrigerate to marinate overnight.
- Remove the pork chops from the bag and shake off to remove the excess marinade.
- Press *Power* button of "Ninja Foodi Digital Air Fry Oven" and turn the dial to select the "Air Broil" mode. Press the *Temp/Darkness* button and use the dial to select HI. To set the temperature, press the *Temp/Darkness* button again.
- Press *Time/Slice* button and again turn the dial to set the cooking time to 15 minutes. Press *Start/Pause* button to start your Air Fry Oven.
- When the unit beeps to show that it is preheated, open the oven door. Place the pork chops over the wire rack and insert in oven.
- After 8 minutes of cooking, flip the chops once. Once the cooking time is completed, open the oven door and serve hot with steamed broccoli.

Nutrition Values Per Serving: Calories: 700; Fat: 59.3g; Sat Fat: 18.3g; Carbs: 2.1g; Fiber: 0.4g; Sugar: 0.3g; Protein: 38.7g

Fried Za'atar Pork Chops

Ingredients for Serving: 8

8 pork loin chops, bone-in

3 garlic cloves, crushed.

2 tbsp. lemon juice

1 tbsp. Za'atar

1 tsp. avocado oil.

1 ¼ tsp. salt

Black pepper, to taste.

Directions and Ready in About: 35-Minutes.

- Rub the pork chops with oil, za'atar, salt, lemon juice, garlic and black pepper. Place these chops in the air fry basket. Transfer the basket to the "Ninja Foodi Digital Air Fry Oven" and close the door.
- Select *Air Fry* mode by rotating the dial. Press the *Time/Slice* button and change the value to 20 minutes. Press the *Temp/Darkness* button and change the value to 400 Degrees °F or (204 Degrees °C).
- Press *Start/Pause* to begin cooking. Flip the chops when cooked halfway through, then resume cooking. Serve warm with mashed potatoes.

Nutrition Values Per Serving: Calories: 437; Fat: 20g; Carbs: 5.1g; Fiber: 0.9g; Sugar: 1.4g; Protein: 37.8g

Rosemary Lamb Chops

Ingredients for Serving: 2

2 garlic cloves, minced.

4 (4-ounce) lamb chops

1 tbsp. olive oil, divided.

1 tbsp. fresh rosemary, chopped.

Salt and ground black pepper, to taste.

Directions and Ready in About: 16-Minutes.

- Take a large bowl, mix together the oil, garlic, rosemary, salt and black pepper. Coat the chops with half of the garlic mixture.

- Press *Power* button of "Ninja Foodi Digital Air Fry Oven" and turn the dial to select *Air Fry* mode. Press *Time/Slice* button and again turn the dial to set the cooking time to 6 minutes.
- Now, push *Temp/Darkness* button and rotate the dial to set the temperature at 390 Degrees °F or (199 Degrees °C). Press *Start/Pause* button to start your Air Fry Oven.
- When the unit beeps to show that it is preheated, open the oven door and grease the air fry basket. Place the lamb chops into the prepared air fry basket and insert in the oven.
- Flip the chops once halfway through. When cooking time is completed, open the oven door and serve hot with the topping of the remaining garlic mixture and with yogurt sauce.

Nutrition Values Per Serving: Calories: 492; Fat: 23.9g; Sat Fat: 7.1g; Carbs: 2.1g; Fiber: 0.8g; Sugar: 0g; Protein: 64g

Garlic Braised Ribs

Ingredients for Serving: 8

5 lbs. bone-in short ribs.	4 sprigs thyme
¼ cup dry red wine	1 cup parsley, chopped.
¼ cup beef stock	½ cup chives, chopped.
1 medium onion, chopped.	2 tbsp. vegetable oil
4 ribs celery, chopped.	3 tbsp. tomato paste
2 medium carrots, chopped.	1 tbsp. lemon zest, grated.
2 heads garlic, halved	Salt and black pepper, to taste.

Directions and Ready in About: 35-Minutes.

- Toss everything in a large bowl, then add short ribs. Mix well to soak the ribs and marinate for 30 minutes. Transfer the soaked ribs to the baking pan and add the marinade around them. Transfer the pan to the "Ninja Foodi Digital Air Fry Oven" and close the door.
- Select *Air Fry* mode by rotating the dial. Press the *Time/Slice* button and change the value to 20 minutes. Press the *Temp/Darkness* button and change the value to 400 Degrees °F or (204 Degrees °C). Press *Start/Pause* to begin cooking. Serve warm with mashed potatoes.

Nutrition Values Per Serving: Calories: 441; Fat: 5g; Sodium: 88mg; Carbs: 13g; Fiber: 0g; Sugar: 0g; Protein: 24g

Garlicky Lamb Chops

Ingredients for Serving: 8

8 medium lamb chops.	1 tsp. dried oregano
2 garlic cloves, crushed	1 tsp. salt
¼ cup olive oil	½ tsp. black pepper.
3 thin lemon slices.	

Directions and Ready in About: 1 hr.

- Place the medium lamb chops in a sheet pan and rub them with olive oil. Add lemon slices, garlic, oregano, salt

and black pepper on top of the lamb chops. Transfer the tray to the "Ninja Foodi Digital Air Fry Oven" and close the door. Select "Air Roast" mode by rotating the dial.
- Press the *Time/Slice* button and change the value to 45 minutes. Press the *Temp/Darkness* button and change the value to 400 Degrees °F or (204 Degrees °C). Press *Start/Pause* to begin cooking. Serve warm with boiled rice or cucumber salad.

Nutrition Values Per Serving: Calories: 461; Fat: 16g; Carbs: 3g; Fiber: 0.1g; Sugar: 1.2g; Protein: 21.3g

Stuffed Bell Peppers with Pork

Ingredients for Serving: 4

⅔ lb. ground pork.	2 cups cooked white rice
1½ cups marinara sauce, divided.	1 tsp. Worcestershire sauce.
½ cup mozzarella cheese, shredded.	1 tsp. Italian seasoning
4 medium green bell peppers	Salt and ground black pepper, to taste.

Directions and Ready in About: 1 hr. 30-Minutes.

- Cut the tops from bell peppers and then carefully remove the seeds. Heat a large skillet over medium heat and cook the pork for about 6-8 minutes. Mince the pork.
- Add the rice, ¾ cup of marinara sauce, Worcestershire sauce, Italian seasoning, salt and black pepper and stir to combine. Remove from the heat. Arrange the bell peppers into the greased sheet pan.
- Carefully, stuff each bell pepper with the pork mixture and top each with the remaining sauce.
- Press *Power* button of "Ninja Foodi Digital Air Fry Oven" and turn the dial to select the *Bake* mode. Press *Time/Slice* button and again turn the dial to set the cooking time to 60 minutes.
- Now, push *Temp/Darkness* button and rotate the dial to set the temperature at 350 Degrees °F or (176 Degrees °C). Press *Start/Pause* button to start your Air Fry Oven. When the unit beeps to show that it is preheated, open the oven door.
- Insert the sheet pan in oven. After 50 minutes of cooking, top each bell pepper with cheese. When cooking time is completed, open the oven door and transfer the bell peppers onto a platter. Serve warm with baby greens.

Nutrition Values Per Serving: Calories: 580; Fat: 7.1g; Sat Fat: 2.2g; Carbs: 96.4g; Fiber: 5.2g; Sugar: 14.8g; Protein: 30.3g

Beef Short Ribs

Ingredients for Serving: 4

1⅔ lbs. short ribs.	1 tsp. ground cumin
¼ cup panko crumbs	½ tsp. orange zest.
1 egg, beaten	1 tsp. grated garlic
1 tsp. avocado oil.	½ tsp. salt
1 tsp. cumin seeds	Salt and black pepper, to taste.

Directions and Ready in About: 50-Minutes.

- Place the beef ribs in a sheet pan and pour the whisked egg on top. Whisk the rest of the crusting ingredients in a bowl and spread over the beef. Transfer the pan to the "Ninja Foodi Digital Air Fry Oven" and close the door.
- Select *Air Fry* mode by rotating the dial. Press the *Time/Slice* button and change the value to 35 minutes. Press the *Temp/Darkness* button and change the value to 350 Degrees °F or (176 Degrees °C). Press *Start/Pause* to begin cooking. Serve warm with white rice or warmed bread.

Nutrition Values Per Serving: Calories: 425; Fat: 14g; Sodium: 411mg; Carbs: 44g; Fiber: 0.3g; Sugar: 1g; Protein: 23g

Buttered Strip Steak

Ingredients for Serving: 4

2 (14-ounce) New York strip steaks.

2 tbsp. butter, melted

Salt and ground black pepper, to taste.

Directions and Ready in About: 25-Minutes.

- Brush each steak with the melted butter evenly and then season with salt and black pepper. Press *Power* button of "Ninja Foodi Digital Air Fry Oven" and turn the dial to select the "Air Broil" mode.
- Press the *Temp/Darkness* button and use the dial to select HI. To set the temperature, press the *Temp/Darkness* button again.
- Press *Time/Slice* button and again turn the dial to set the cooking time to 15 minutes. Press *Start/Pause* button to start your Air Fry Oven. When the unit beeps to show that it is preheated, open the oven door.
- Place the steaks over the wire rack and insert in oven. When cooking time is completed, open the oven door and place the steaks onto a cutting board for about 5 minutes before slicing.
- Cut each steak into 2 portions and serve alongside with the spiced potatoes.

Nutrition Values Per Serving: Calories: 296; Fat: 12.7g; Sat Fat: 6.6g; Carbs: 0g; Fiber: 0g; Sugar: 0g; Protein: 44.5g

Lamb Chops with Carrots

Ingredients for Serving: 4

4 (6-ounce) lamb chops.

2 large carrots, peeled and cubed

1 garlic clove, minced.

3 tbsp. olive oil

2 tbsp. fresh mint leaves, minced.

2 tbsp. fresh rosemary, minced.

Salt and ground black pepper, to taste.

Directions and Ready in About: 25-Minutes.

- Take a large bowl, mix together the herbs, garlic, oil, salt and black pepper. Add the chops and generously coat with mixture. Refrigerate to marinate for about 3 hours.
- In a large pan of water, soak the carrots for about 15 minutes. Drain the carrots completely.

- Press *Power* button of "Ninja Foodi Digital Air Fry Oven" and turn the dial to select *Air Fry* mode. Press *Time/Slice* button and again turn the dial to set the cooking time to 10 minutes.
- Now, push *Temp/Darkness* button and rotate the dial to set the temperature at 390 Degrees °F or (199 Degrees °C). Press *Start/Pause* button to start your Air Fry Oven.
- When the unit beeps to show that it is preheated, open the oven door. Arrange chops into the greased air fry basket in a single layer and insert in the oven.
- After 2 minutes of cooking, arrange carrots into the air fry basket and top with the chops in a single layer. Insert the basket in oven. Once the cooking time is completed, open the oven door and transfer the chops and carrots onto serving plates. Serve hot with fresh greens.

Nutrition Values Per Serving: Calories: 429; Fat: 23.2g; Sat Fat: 6.1g; Carbs: 5.1g; Fiber: 1.8g; Sugar: 1.8g; Protein: 48.3g

Herbed Chuck Roast

Ingredients for Serving: 6

1 (2-pound) beef chuck roast.

1 tsp. dried thyme, crushed.

1 tbsp. olive oil

1 tsp. dried rosemary, crushed

Salt, to taste.

Directions and Ready in About: 55-Minutes.

- Take a bowl, add the oil, herbs and salt and mix well. Coat the beef roast with herb mixture generously. Arrange the beef roast onto the greased sheet pan.
- Press *Power* button of "Ninja Foodi Digital Air Fry Oven" and turn the dial to select *Air Fry* mode. Press *Time/Slice* button and again turn the dial to set the cooking time to 45 minutes.
- Now, push *Temp/Darkness* button and rotate the dial to set the temperature at 360 Degrees °F or (182 Degrees °C). Press *Start/Pause* button to start your Air Fry Oven. When the unit beeps to show that it is preheated, open the oven door and insert the sheet pan in the oven.
- When cooking time is completed, open the oven door and place the roast onto a cutting board. With a piece of foil, cover the beef roast for about 20 minutes before slicing.
- With a sharp knife, cut the beef roast into desired size slices and serve with roasted Brussels sprouts.

Nutrition Values Per Serving: Calories: 304; Fat: 14g; Sat Fat: 4.5g; Carbs: 0.2g; Fiber: 0.2g; Sugar: 0g; Protein: 41.5g

Mint Lamb with Toasted Hazelnuts

Ingredients for Serving: 2

⅔ lb. shoulder lamb, cut into strips

½ cup white wine

¼ cup hazelnuts, toasted

½ cup frozen peas

¼ cup water

2 tbsp. mint leaves, chopped.

1 tbsp. hazelnut oil

Salt and black pepper to taste.

Directions and Ready in About: 40-Minutes.

- Toss lamb with hazelnuts, spices and all the ingredients in a sheet pan. Transfer the pan to the "Ninja Foodi Digital Air Fry Oven" and close the door. Select *Bake* mode by rotating the dial. Press the *Time/Slice* button and change the value to 25 minutes.
- Press the *Temp/Darkness* button and change the value to 370 Degrees °F or (187 Degrees °C). Press *Start/Pause* to begin cooking. Serve warm with carrots and potatoes on the side.

Nutrition Values Per Serving: Calories: 445; Fat: 36g; Carbs: 1g; Fiber: 0.2g; Sugar: 0.1g; Protein: 22.5g

Lamb Burgers

Ingredients for Serving: 6

2 lbs. ground lamb.	¼ tsp. ground cumin
½ tbsp. garlic powder	Salt and ground black pepper, to taste.
½ tbsp. onion powder.	

Directions and Ready in About: 18-Minutes.

- Take a bowl, add all the ingredients and mix well. Make 6 equal-sized patties from the mixture. Arrange the patties onto the greased sheet pan in a single layer.
- Press *Power* button of "Ninja Foodi Digital Air Fry Oven" and turn the dial to select *Air Fry* mode. Press *Time/Slice* button and again turn the dial to set the cooking time to 8 minutes.
- Now, push *Temp/Darkness* button and rotate the dial to set the temperature at 360 Degrees °F or (182 Degrees °C). Press *Start/Pause* button to start your Air Fry Oven.
- When the unit beeps to show that it is preheated, open the oven door. Insert the sheet pan in oven. Flip the burgers once halfway through. When cooking time is completed, open the oven door and serve hot with fresh salad.

Nutrition Values Per Serving: Calories: 286; Fat: 11.1g; Sat Fat: 4g; Carbs: 1g; Fiber: 0.1g; Sugar: 0.4g; Protein: 42.7g

Bacon Wrapped Pork Tenderloin

Ingredients for Serving: 4

1 (1½-pound) pork tenderloin.	1 tbsp. honey
4 bacon strips	2 tbsp. Dijon mustard.

Directions and Ready in About: 45-Minutes.

- Coat the tenderloin with mustard and honey. Wrap the pork tenderloin with bacon strips.
- Press *Power* button of "Ninja Foodi Digital Air Fry Oven" and turn the dial to select *Air Fry* mode. Press *Time/Slice* button and again turn the dial to set the cooking time to 30 minutes.
- Now, push *Temp/Darkness* button and rotate the dial to set the temperature at 360 Degrees °F or (182 Degrees °C). Press *Start/Pause* button to start your Air Fry Oven. When the unit beeps to show that it is preheated, open the oven door and grease the air fry basket.

- Place the pork tenderloin into the prepared air fry basket and insert in the oven. Flip the pork tenderloin once halfway through.
- When cooking time is completed, open the oven door and place the pork loin onto a cutting board for about 10 minutes before slicing. With a sharp knife, cut the tenderloin into desired sized slices and serve with mashed potatoes.

Nutrition Values Per Serving: Calories: 386; Fat: 16.1g; Sat Fat: 5.7g; Carbs: 4.8g; Fiber: 0.3g; Sugar: 4.4g; Protein: 52g

Minced Lamb Casserole

Ingredients for Serving: 6

½ lb. ground lamb	1 cup small pasta shells, cooked.
4 fresh mushrooms, sliced.	2 cups bottled marinara sauce
1 cup milk	
1 egg, beaten	2 tbsp. olive oil
1 medium onion, chopped.	1 tsp. butter
1 cup cheddar cheese, grated.	4 tsp. flour.

Directions and Ready in About: 46-Minutes.

- Put a wok on moderate heat and add oil to heat. Toss in onion and sauté until soft. Stir in mushrooms and lamb, then cook until meat is brown. Add marinara sauce and cook it to a simmer. Stir in pasta, then spread this mixture in a casserole dish.
- Prepare the sauce by melting butter in a suitable saucepan over moderate heat. Stir in flour and whisk well, pour in the milk. Mix well and whisk ¼ cup of sauce with egg, then return it to the saucepan.
- Stir, cook for 1 minute, then pour this sauce over the lamb. Drizzle cheese over the lamb casserole. Transfer the dish to the "Ninja Foodi Digital Air Fry Oven" and close the door.
- Select *Bake* mode by rotating the dial. Press the *Time/Slice* button and change the value to 30 minutes. Press the *Temp/Darkness* button and change the value to 350 Degrees °F or (176 Degrees °C). Press *Start/Pause* to begin cooking. Serve warm with quinoa salad.

Nutrition Values Per Serving: Calories: 448; Fat: 23g; Sodium: 350mg; Carbs: 18g; Fiber: 6.3g; Sugar: 1g; Protein: 40.3g

Easy Pork Chops

Ingredients for Serving: 2

2 (6-ounce) (½-inch thick) pork chops	Salt and ground black pepper, to taste.

Directions and Ready in About: 28-Minutes.

- Season the pork chops with salt and black pepper evenly. Arrange the pork chops onto a greased sheet pan.
- Press *Power* button of "Ninja Foodi Digital Air Fry Oven" and turn the dial to select the "Air Broil" mode. Press the *Temp/Darkness* button and use the dial to select HI. To set the temperature, press the *Temp/Darkness* button again.

- Press *Time/Slice* button and again turn the dial to set the cooking time to 18 minutes. Press *Start/Pause* button to start your Air Fry Oven. When the unit beeps to show that it is preheated, open the oven door and insert the sheet pan in oven.
- After 12 minutes of cooking, flip the chops once. When cooking time is completed, open the oven door and serve hot alongside with the mashed potato.

Nutrition Values Per Serving: Calories: 544; Fat: 42.3g; Sat Fat: 15.8g; Carbs: 0g; Fiber: 0g; Sugar: 0g; Protein: 38.2g

Greek lamb Farfalle

Ingredients for Serving: 6

¾ lb. tin tomatoes, chopped.	1 ball half-fat mozzarella, torn
1 lb. pack lamb mince	2 garlic cloves, chopped.
¼ cup black olives pitted.	½ cup frozen spinach, defrosted
1 onion, chopped.	
9 oz. farfalle paste, boiled.	1 tbsp. olive oil
2 tbsp. dill, removed and chopped	2 tsp. dried oregano.

Directions and Ready in About: 35-Minutes.

- Sauté onion and garlic with oil in a pan over moderate heat for 5 minutes. Stir in tomatoes, spinach, dill, oregano, lamb and olives, then stir cook for 5 minutes. Spread the lamb in a casserole dish and toss in the boiled Farfalle pasta. Top the pasta lamb mix with mozzarella cheese. Transfer the dish to the "Ninja Foodi Digital Air Fry Oven" and close the door.
- Select *Air Fry* mode by rotating the dial. Press the *Time/Slice* button and change the value to 10 minutes. Press the *Temp/Darkness* button and change the value to 350 Degrees °F or (176 Degrees °C). Press *Start/Pause* to begin cooking. Serve warm with fresh green and mashed potatoes.

Nutrition Values Per Serving: Calories: 461; Fat: 5g; Sodium: 340mg; Carbs: 24.7g; Fiber: 1.2g; Sugar: 1.3g; Protein: 15.3g

Steak with Bell Peppers

Ingredients for Serving: 4

1¼ lbs. flank steak, cut into thin strips.	1 tsp. garlic powder.
3 green bell peppers, seeded and cubed	1 tsp. red chili powder
1 red onion, sliced.	1 tsp. dried oregano, crushed.
3-4 tbsp. feta cheese, crumbled	1 tsp. onion powder
2 tbsp. olive oil	1 tsp. paprika
	Salt, to taste.

Directions and Ready in About: 26-Minutes.

- Take a large bowl, mix together the oregano and spices. Add the steak strips, bell peppers, onion and oil and mix until well combined.

- Press *Power* button of "Ninja Foodi Digital Air Fry Oven" and turn the dial to select *Air Fry* mode. Press *Time/Slice* button and again turn the dial to set the cooking time to 11 minutes.
- Now, push *Temp/Darkness* button and rotate the dial to set the temperature at 390 Degrees °F or (199 Degrees °C). Press *Start/Pause* button to start your Air Fry Oven. When the unit beeps to show that it is preheated, open the oven door and grease the air fry basket.
- Place the steak mixture into the prepared air fry basket and insert in the oven. When cooking time is completed, open the oven door and transfer the steak mixture onto serving plates. Serve immediately with the topping of feta and with plain rice.

Nutrition Values Per Serving: Calories: 732; Fat: 35g; Sat Fat: 12.9g; Carbs: 11.5g; Fiber: 2.5g; Sugar: 6.5g; Protein: 89.3g

Beef Zucchini Shashliks

Ingredients for Serving: 4

1 lb. beef, boned and diced	3 green peppers, cubed.
20 garlic cloves, chopped.	2 zucchinis, cubed.
1 handful rosemary, chopped.	1 lime, juiced and chopped
2 red onions, cut into wedges	3 tbsp. olive oil

Directions and Ready in About: 40-Minutes.

- Toss the beef with the rest of the skewer's ingredients in a bowl. Thread the beef, peppers, zucchini and onion on the skewers. Place these beef skewers in the air fry basket. Transfer the basket to the "Ninja Foodi Digital Air Fry Oven" and close the door.
- Select *Air Fry* mode by rotating the dial. Press the *Time/Slice* button and change the value to 25 minutes. Press the *Temp/Darkness* button and change the value to 370 Degrees °F or (187 Degrees °C).
- Press *Start/Pause* to begin cooking. Flip the skewers when cooked halfway through, then resume cooking. Serve warm with crispy bacon and sautéed vegetables.

Nutrition Values Per Serving: Calories: 416; Fat: 21g; Sodium: 476mg; Carbs: 22g; Fiber: 3g; Sugar: 4g; Protein: 20g

Garlicky Lamb Steaks

Ingredients for Serving: 4

1½ lbs. boneless lamb sirloin steaks.	½ tsp. ground cumin
½ onion, roughly chopped	½ tsp. ground cinnamon.
5 garlic cloves, peeled.	½ tsp. cayenne pepper
1 tbsp. fresh ginger, peeled.	Salt and ground black pepper, to taste.
1 tsp. ground fennel	

Directions and Ready in About: 30-Minutes.

- In a blender, add the onion, garlic, ginger and spices and pulse until smooth. Transfer the mixture into a large bowl. Add the lamb steaks and coat with the mixture generously. Refrigerate to marinate for about 24 hours.

- Press *Power* button of "Ninja Foodi Digital Air Fry Oven" and turn the dial to select *Air Fry* mode. Press *Time/Slice* button and again turn the dial to set the cooking time to 15 minutes.
- Now, push *Temp/Darkness* button and rotate the dial to set the temperature at 330 Degrees °F or (166 Degrees °C). Press *Start/Pause* button to start your Air Fry Oven. When the unit beeps to show that it is preheated, open the oven door and grease the air fry basket.
- Place the lamb steaks into the prepared air fry basket and insert in the oven. Flip the steaks once halfway through. When cooking time is completed, open the oven door and serve hot with your favorite greens.

Nutrition Values Per Serving: Calories: 336; Fat: 12.8g; Sat Fat: 4.5g; Carbs: 4.2g; Fiber: 1g; Sugar: 0.7g; Protein: 8.4g

Sauce Glazed Meatloaf

Ingredients for Serving: 6

1 lb. ground beef.	1 ½ tbsp. ketchup
¼ cup breadcrumbs	2 tbsp. milk
1 ½ garlic clove, minced.	1 ½ tsp. herb seasoning.
½ onion chopped	¼ tsp. black pepper
1 egg	½ tsp. ground paprika
1 ½ tbsp. fresh parsley, chopped.	Salt to taste

Glaze:

¾ cup ketchup	1 ½ tsp. white vinegar
2 ½ tbsp. brown sugar	½ tsp. onion powder
¼ tsp. ground black pepper.	1 tsp. garlic powder.
	¼ tsp. salt

Directions and Ready in About: 1 hr. 15-Minutes.

- Thoroughly mix ground beef with egg, onion, garlic, crumbs and all the ingredients in a bowl. Grease a meatloaf pan with oil or butter and spread the minced beef in the pan. Transfer the pan to the "Ninja Foodi Digital Air Fry Oven" and close the door.
- Select *Air Fry* mode by rotating the dial. Press the *Time/Slice* button and change value to 40 minutes Press the *Temp/Darkness* button and change the value to 375 Degrees °F or (190 Degrees °C).
- Press *Start/Pause* to begin cooking. Meanwhile, prepare the glaze by whisking its ingredients in a suitable saucepan.
- Stir cook for 5 minutes until it thickens. Brush this glaze over the meatloaf and bake it again for 15 minutes. Slice and serve with mashed potatoes.

Nutrition Values Per Serving: Calories: 435; Fat: 25g; Sodium: 532mg; Carbs: 23g; Fiber: 0.4g; Sugar: 2g; Protein: 28.3g

Lamb Chops with Rosemary Sauce

Ingredients for Serving: 8

8 lamb loin chops	Salt and black pepper, to taste.
1 small onion, peeled and chopped.	

For the sauce:

1 oz. plain flour.	6 oz. milk
1 oz. butter	2 tbsp. cream, whipping.
1 onion, peeled and chopped.	1 tbsp. rosemary leaves
6 oz. vegetable stock	Salt and black pepper, to taste.

Directions and Ready in About: 1 hr.

- Place the lamb loin chops and onion in a sheet pan, then drizzle salt and black pepper on top. Transfer the pan to the "Ninja Foodi Digital Air Fry Oven" and close the door.
- Select *Air Fry* mode by rotating the dial. Press the *Time/Slice* button and change the value to 45 minutes. Press the *Temp/Darkness* button and change the value to 350 Degrees °F or (176 Degrees °C).
- Press *Start/Pause* to begin cooking. Prepare the white sauce by melting butter in a suitable saucepan, then stir in onions.
- Sauté for 5 minutes, then stir flour and stir cook for 2 minutes. Stir in the rest of the ingredients and mix well. Pour the sauce over baked chops and serve with a fresh greens salad.

Nutrition Values Per Serving: Calories: 450; Fat: 20g; Sodium: 686mg; Carbs: 3g; Fiber: 1g; Sugar: 1.2g; Protein: 31g

Fish and Seafood Recipes

Salmon with Prawns

Ingredients for Serving: 4

½ lb. cherry tomatoes, chopped.

8 large prawns, peeled and deveined

4 (4-ounce) salmon fillets.

2 tbsp. olive oil

2 tbsp. fresh thyme, chopped.

2 tbsp. fresh lemon juice

Directions and Ready in About: 33-Minutes.

- In the bottom of a greased baking pan, place salmon fillets and tomatoes in a greased baking dish in a single layer and drizzle with the oil.
- Arrange the prawns on top in a single layer. Drizzle with lemon juice and sprinkle with thyme.
- Press *Power* button of "Ninja Foodi Digital Air Fry Oven" and turn the dial to select *Air Fry* mode. Press *Time/Slice* button and again turn the dial to set the cooking time to 18 minutes.
- Now, push *Temp/Darkness* button and rotate the dial to set the temperature at 390 Degrees °F or (199 Degrees °C).
- Press *Start/Pause* button to start your Air Fry Oven. When the unit beeps to show that it is preheated, open the oven door.
- Arrange the baking pan into the air fry basket and insert in the oven. When cooking time is completed, open the oven door and serve immediately with pasta of your choice.

Nutrition Values Per Serving: Calories: 239; Fat: 14.5g; Sat Fat: 2.2g; Carbs: 3.4g; Fiber: 1.2g; Sugar: 1.7g; Protein: 25.2g

Salmon Burgers

Ingredients for Serving: 6

1 (6-ounce) cooked salmon fillet.

¾ cup frozen vegetables (of your choice), parboiled and drained.

3 large russet potatoes, peeled and cubed

1 cup breadcrumbs.

¼ cup olive oil

1 egg

2 tbsp. fresh parsley, chopped.

1 tsp. fresh dill, chopped.

Salt and ground black pepper, to taste.

- Directions and Ready in About: 37-Minutes.
- In a pan of boiling water, cook the potatoes for about 10 minutes. Drain the potatoes well.
- Transfer the potatoes into a bowl and mash with a potato masher. Set aside to cool completely.
- In another bowl, add the salmon and flake with a fork. Add the cooked potatoes, egg, parboiled vegetables, parsley, dill, salt and black pepper and mix until well combined.
- Make 6 equal-sized patties from the mixture. Coat patties with breadcrumb evenly and then drizzle with the oil evenly.

- Press *Power* button of "Ninja Foodi Digital Air Fry Oven" and turn the dial to select *Air Fry* mode. Press *Time/Slice* button and again turn the dial to set the cooking time to 12 minutes.
- Now, push *Temp/Darkness* button and rotate the dial to set the temperature at 355 Degrees °F or (179 Degrees °C).
- Press *Start/Pause* button to start your Air Fry Oven. When the unit beeps to show that it is preheated, open the oven door.
- Arrange the patties in greased air fry basket and insert in the oven. Flip the patties once halfway through.
- When cooking time is completed, open the oven door and serve hot with your favorite dipping sauce.

Nutrition Values Per Serving: Calories: 334; Fat: 12.1g; Sat Fat: 2g; Carbs: 45.2g; Fiber: 6.3g; Sugar: 4g; Protein: 12.5g

Pesto Salmon

Ingredients for Serving: 4

1¼ lbs. salmon fillet, cut into 4 fillets.

1 tbsp. fresh lemon juice

2 tbsp. white wine.

2 tbsp. pesto

Directions and Ready in About: 30-Minutes.

- Arrange the salmon fillets onto q foil-lined sheet pan, skin-side down. Drizzle the salmon fillets with wine and lemon juice. Set aside for about 15 minutes. Spread pesto over each salmon fillet evenly.
- Press *Power* button of "Ninja Foodi Digital Air Fry Oven" and turn the dial to select the "Air Broil" mode. Press *Time/Slice* button and again turn the dial to set the cooking time to 15 minutes.
- Press *Temp/Darkness* button and turn the dial to set HI. To set the temperature, press the *Temp/Darkness* button again.
- Press *Start/Pause* button to start your Air Fry Oven. When the unit beeps to show that it is preheated, open the oven door.
- Insert the sheet pan in oven. When cooking time is completed, open the oven door and serve hot with lemon slices.

Nutrition Values Per Serving: Calories: 228; Fat: 12g; Sat Fat: 1.9g; Carbs: 0.8g; Fiber: 0.2g; Sugar: 0.6g; Protein: 28.3g

Lemony Salmon

Ingredients for Serving: 3

1½ lbs. salmon.

1 lemon, cut into slices

1 tbsp. fresh dill, chopped.

½ tsp. red chili powder

Salt and ground black pepper, to taste.

Directions and Ready in About: 18-Minutes.

- Season the salmon with chili powder, salt and black pepper. Press *Power* button of "Ninja Foodi Digital Air Fry Oven" and turn the dial to select *Air Fry* mode.
- Press *Time/Slice* button and again turn the dial to set the cooking time to 8 minutes.

- Now, push *Temp/Darkness* button and rotate the dial to set the temperature at 375 Degrees °F or (190 Degrees °C).
- Press *Start/Pause* button to start your Air Fry Oven. When the unit beeps to show that it is preheated, open the oven door.
- Arrange the salmon fillets into the greased air fry basket and insert in the oven. When cooking time is completed, open the oven door and serve hot with the garnishing of fresh dill. Serve with the topping of cheese.

Nutrition Values Per Serving: Calories: 305; Fat: 14.1g; Sat Fat: 2g; Carbs: 1.3g; Fiber: 0.4g; Sugar: 0.2g; Protein: 44.3g

Cajun Salmon

Ingredients for Serving: 2

2 (7-ounce) (¾-inch thick) salmon fillets.

1 tbsp. fresh lemon juice

1 tbsp. Cajun seasoning.

½ tsp. sugar

Directions and Ready in About: 17-Minutes.

- Sprinkle the salmon fillets with Cajun seasoning and sugar evenly.
- Press *Power* button of "Ninja Foodi Digital Air Fry Oven" and turn the dial to select *Air Fry* mode. Press *Time/Slice* button and again turn the dial to set the cooking time to 7 minutes.
- Now, push *Temp/Darkness* button and rotate the dial to set the temperature at 355 Degrees °F or (179 Degrees °C).
- Press *Start/Pause* button to start your Air Fry Oven. When the unit beeps to show that it is preheated, open the oven door.
- Arrange the salmon fillets, skin-side up in the greased air fry basket and insert in the oven. When cooking time is completed, open the oven door and transfer the salmon fillets onto a platter. Drizzle with the lemon juice and serve hot with mashed cauliflower.

Nutrition Values Per Serving: Calories: 268; Fat: 12.3g; Sat Fat: 1.8g; Carbs: 1.2g; Fiber: 0g; Sugar: 1.2g; Protein: 36.8g

Crispy Catfish

Ingredients for Serving: 5

5 (6-ounce) catfish fillets.

¼ cup all-purpose flour

½ cup cornmeal.

½ cup yellow mustard

1 cup milk

2 tbsp. dried parsley flakes.

2 tsp. fresh lemon juice

¼ tsp. red chili powder.

¼ tsp. cayenne pepper

¼ tsp. onion powder.

¼ tsp. garlic powder

Olive oil cooking spray.

Salt and ground black pepper, to taste.

Directions and Ready in About: 30-Minutes.

- Take a large bowl, place the catfish, milk and lemon juice and refrigerate for about 15 minutes. Take a shallow bowl, add the mustard.

- In another bowl, mix together the cornmeal, flour, parsley flakes and spices. Remove the catfish fillets from milk mixture and with paper towels, pat them dry.
- Coat each fish fillet with mustard and then roll into cornmeal mixture.
- Then, spray each fillet with the cooking spray. Press *Power* button of "Ninja Foodi Digital Air Fry Oven" and turn the dial to select *Air Fry* mode. Press *Time/Slice* button and again turn the dial to set the cooking time to 15 minutes.
- Now, push *Temp/Darkness* button and rotate the dial to set the temperature at 400 Degrees °F or (204 Degrees °C).
- Press *Start/Pause* button to start your Air Fry Oven. When the unit beeps to show that it is preheated, open the oven door.
- Arrange the catfish fillets into the greased air fry basket and insert in the oven.
- After 10 minutes of cooking, flip the fillets and spray with the cooking spray. When cooking time is completed, open the oven door and serve hot with cheese sauce.

Nutrition Values Per Serving: Calories: 340; Fat: 15.5g; Sat Fat: 3.1g; Carbs: 18.3g; Fiber: 2g; Sugar: 2.7g; Protein: 30.9g

Nuts Crusted Salmon

Ingredients for Serving: 2

2 (6-ounce) skinless salmon fillets.

3 tbsp. quick-cooking oats, crushed

2 tbsp. olive oil

3 tbsp. walnuts, chopped finely.

Salt and ground black pepper, to taste.

Directions and Ready in About: 30-Minutes.

- Rub the salmon fillets with salt and black pepper evenly. Take a bowl, mix together the walnuts, oats and oil.
- Arrange the salmon fillets onto the greased sheet pan in a single layer. Place the oat mixture over salmon fillets and gently, press down.
- Press *Power* button of "Ninja Foodi Digital Air Fry Oven" and turn the dial to select the *Bake* mode. Press *Time/Slice* button and again turn the dial to set the cooking time to 15 minutes.
- Now, push *Temp/Darkness* button and rotate the dial to set the temperature at 400 Degrees °F or (204 Degrees °C).
- Press *Start/Pause* button to start your Air Fry Oven. When the unit beeps to show that it is preheated, open the oven door.
- Insert the sheet pan in oven. When cooking time is completed, open the oven door and serve hot with steamed asparagus.

Nutrition Values Per Serving: Calories: 446; Fat: 319g; Sat Fat: 4g; Carbs: 6.4g; Fiber: 1.6g; Sugar: 0.2g; Protein: 36.8g

Tangy Sea Bass

Ingredients for Serving: 2

2 (5-ounce) sea bass fillets.

1 garlic clove, minced.

1 tbsp. balsamic vinegar

1 tbsp. olive oil

1 tsp. fresh dill, minced.

Salt and ground black pepper, to taste.

Directions and Ready in About: 22-Minutes.

- In a large resealable bag, add all the ingredients. Seal the bag and shake well to mix. Refrigerate to marinate for at least 30 minutes.
- Remove the fish fillets from bag and shake off the excess marinade. Arrange the fish fillets onto the greased sheet pan in a single layer.
- Press *Power* button of "Ninja Foodi Digital Air Fry Oven" and turn the dial to select *Bake* mode. Press *Time/Slice* button and again turn the dial to set the cooking time to 12 minutes.
- Now, push *Temp/Darkness* button and rotate the dial to set the temperature at 450 Degrees °F or (232 Degrees °C).
- Press *Start/Pause* button to start your Air Fry Oven. When the unit beeps to show that it is preheated, open the oven door and insert the sheet pan in oven.
- Open the Flip the fish fillets once halfway through. When cooking time is completed, open the oven door and serve hot with fresh salad.

Nutrition Values Per Serving: Calories: 241; Fat: 10.7g; Sat Fat: 1.9g; Carbs: 0.9g; Fiber: 0.1g; Sugar: 0.1g; Protein: 33.7g

White Sauce Cod

Ingredients for Serving: 4

2 (4-ounce) cod fillets.

¼ cup champagne

¼ cup white sauce.

1 tsp. oil

6 asparagus stalks

Salt and ground black pepper, to taste.

Directions and Ready in About: 33-Minutes.

- Take a bowl, mix together all the ingredients. Divide the cod mixture over 2 pieces of foil evenly. Seal the foil around the cod mixture to form the packet.
- Press *Power* button of "Ninja Foodi Digital Air Fry Oven" and turn the dial to select *Air Fry* mode. Press *Time/Slice* button and again turn the dial to set the cooking time to 13 minutes.
- Now, push *Temp/Darkness* button and rotate the dial to set the temperature at 355 Degrees °F or (179 Degrees °C). Press *Start/Pause* button to start your Air Fry Oven.
- When the unit beeps to show that it is preheated, open the oven door. Arrange the cod parcels in air fry basket and insert in the oven.
- When cooking time is completed, open the oven door and transfer the parcels onto serving plates. Carefully unwrap the parcels and serve hot with mashed potatoes.

Nutrition Values Per Serving: Calories: 188; Fat: 6.6g; Sat Fat: 1.2g; Carbs: 5g; Fiber: 0.8g; Sugar: 2.2g; Protein: 22.2g

Maple Bacon Salmon

Ingredients for Serving: 4

For the Salmon:

1 (2 ¼-pound) skin-on salmon fillet.

1 lemon, sliced.

⅓ cup olive oil

1 tbsp. Dijon mustard.

2 tbsp. lemon juice

2 tbsp. maple syrup

2 ½ tsp. salt, black pepper and garlic seasoning

Chopped chives for garnish.

Candied Bacon

1 tbsp. packed brown sugar

3 tbsp. maple syrup

¼ tsp. salt, black pepper and garlic seasoning.

Directions and Ready in About: 44-Minutes.

- Place lemon slices in a sheet pan and top them with salmon. Drizzle salt, black pepper and garlic seasoning on top. Mix mustard, oil, maple syrup, lemon juice, salt, black pepper and seasoning in a bowl.
- Pour this sauce over the salmon. Transfer the pan to the "Ninja Foodi Digital Air Fry Oven" and close the door.
- Select *Air Fry* mode by rotating the dial. Press the *Time/Slice* button and change the value to 25 minutes.
- Press the *Temp/Darkness* button and change the value to 350 Degrees °F or (176 Degrees °C).
- Press *Start/Pause* to begin cooking. Meanwhile, mix brown sugar, salt, black pepper and garlic seasoning in a bowl.
- Sauté bacon in a skillet until crispy and pour the sugar syrup on top. Cook for 4 minutes until the liquid is absorbed.
- Allow the bacon to cool and then crumble it. Garnish the salmon with crumbled bacon and chopped chives. Serve warm with roasted broccoli florets.

Nutrition Values Per Serving: Calories: 415; Fat: 15g; Carbs: 4.3g; Fiber: 1.4g; Sugar: 1g; Protein: 23.3g

Easy Crispy Cod

Ingredients for Serving: 4

4 (4-ounce) (¾-inch thick) cod fillets.

2 eggs

½ cup panko breadcrumbs.

2 tbsp. all-purpose flour

1 tsp. fresh dill, minced.

½ tsp. dry mustard

½ tsp. onion powder.

½ tsp. lemon zest, grated.

½ tsp. paprika

Salt, to taste.

Olive oil cooking spray

Directions and Ready in About: 30-Minutes.

- Season the cod fillets with salt generously. Take a shallow bowl, place the flour. Crack the eggs in a second bowl and beat well.

- In a third bowl, mix together the panko, dill, lemon zest, mustard and spices. Coat each cod fillet with the flour, then dip into beaten eggs and finally, coat with panko mixture.
- Press *Power* button of "Ninja Foodi Digital Air Fry Oven" and turn the dial to select *Air Fry* mode. Press *Time/Slice* button and again turn the dial to set the cooking time to 15 minutes.
- Now, push *Temp/Darkness* button and rotate the dial to set the temperature at 400 Degrees °F or (204 Degrees °C).
- Press *Start/Pause* button to start your Air Fry Oven. When the unit beeps to show that it is preheated, open the oven door and grease the air fry basket.
- Place the cod fillets into the prepared air fry basket and insert in the oven. Flip the cod fillets once halfway through. When cooking time is completed, open the oven door and serve hot with steamed green beans.

Nutrition Values Per Serving: Calories: 190; Fat: 4.3g; Sat Fat: 1.1g; Carbs: 5.9g; Fiber: 0.4g; Sugar: 0.4g; Protein: 24g

Salmon with Broccoli

Ingredients for Serving: 2

2 (6-ounce) skin-on salmon fillets.

1 (½-inch) piece fresh ginger, grated.

1½ cups small broccoli florets

2 tbsp. vegetable oil, divided.

1 tbsp. soy sauce

1 tsp. light brown sugar.

¼ tsp. cornstarch

1 tsp. rice vinegar

Salt and ground black pepper, to taste.

Directions and Ready in About: 27-Minutes.

- Take a bowl, mix together the broccoli, 1 tbsp. of oil, salt and black pepper. In another bowl, mix well the ginger, soy sauce, vinegar, sugar and cornstarch.
- Coat the salmon fillets with remaining oil and then with the ginger mixture. Press *Power* button of "Ninja Foodi Digital Air Fry Oven" and turn the dial to select *Air Fry* mode.
- Press *Time/Slice* button and again turn the dial to set the cooking time to 12 minutes. Now, push *Temp/Darkness* button and rotate the dial to set the temperature at 375 Degrees °F or (190 Degrees °C).
- Press *Start/Pause* button to start your Air Fry Oven. When the unit beeps to show that it is preheated, open the oven door.
- Arrange the broccoli florets into the greased air fry basket and top with the salmon fillets.
- Insert the basket in the oven. When cooking time is completed, remove basket from oven and cool for 5 minutes before serving. Serve with the garnishing of lemon zest.

Nutrition Values Per Serving: Calories: 385; Fat: 24.4g; Sat Fat: 4.2g; Carbs: 7.8g; Fiber: 2.1g; Sugar: 3g; Protein: 35.6g

Crispy Flounder

Ingredients for Serving: 3

1 cup dry Italian breadcrumb.

3 (6-ounce) flounder fillets

¼ cup olive oil.

1 egg

Directions and Ready in About: 27-Minutes.

- Take a shallow bowl, beat the egg. In another bowl, add the breadcrumbs and oil and mix until a crumbly mixture is formed. Dip the flounder fillets into the beaten egg and then coat with the breadcrumb mixture.
- Press *Power* button of "Ninja Foodi Digital Air Fry Oven" and turn the dial to select *Air Fry* mode. Press *Time/Slice* button and again turn the dial to set the cooking time to 12 minutes.
- Now, push *Temp/Darkness* button and rotate the dial to set the temperature at 355 Degrees °F or (179 Degrees °C).
- Press *Start/Pause* button to start your Air Fry Oven. When the unit beeps to show that it is preheated, open the oven door and grease the air fry basket.
- Place the flounder fillets into the prepared air fry basket and insert in the oven. When cooking time is completed, open the oven door and serve hot with potato chips.

Nutrition Values Per Serving: Calories: 508; Fat: 22.8g; Sat Fat: 3.9g; Carbs: 26.5g; Fiber: 1.8g; Sugar: 2.5g; Protein: 47.8g

Buttered Trout

Ingredients for Serving: 2

2 (6-ounce) trout fillets.

1 tbsp. butter, melted

Salt and ground black pepper, to taste.

Directions and Ready in About: 20-Minutes.

- Season each trout fillet with salt and black pepper and then coat with the butter. Arrange the trout fillets onto the greased sheet pan in a single layer.
- Press *Power* button of "Ninja Foodi Digital Air Fry Oven" and turn the dial to select *Air Fry* mode. Press *Time/Slice* button and again turn the dial to set the cooking time to 10 minutes.
- Now, push *Temp/Darkness* button and rotate the dial to set the temperature at 360 Degrees °F or (182 Degrees °C). Press *Start/Pause* button to start your Air Fry Oven.
- When the unit beeps to show that it is preheated, open the oven door. Insert the sheet pan in oven. Flip the fillets once halfway through. When cooking time is completed, open the oven door and serve hot with your favorite salad.

Nutrition Values Per Serving: Calories: 374; Fat: 20.2g; Sat Fat: 6.2g; Carbs: 0g; Fiber: 0g; Sugar: 0g; Protein: 45.4g

Baked Tilapia with Buttery Crumb

Ingredients for Serving: 4

4 tilapia fillets.

1 cup bread crumbs

3 tbsp. butter, melted.

½ tsp. dried basil

Salt and black pepper to taste.

Directions and Ready in About: 31-Minutes.

- Rub the tilapia fillets with black pepper and salt, then place them in the sheet pan. Mix butter, breadcrumbs and seasonings in a bowl.
- Sprinkle the breadcrumbs mixture on top of the tilapia. Transfer the fish to the "Ninja Foodi Digital Air Fry Oven" and close the door.
- Select *Bake* mode by rotating the dial. Press the *Time/Slice* button and change the value to 15 minutes.
- Press the *Temp/Darkness* button and change the value to 375 Degrees °F or (190 Degrees °C). Press *Start/Pause* to begin cooking. Switch to "AIR BROIL" at "HI" and cook for 1 minute. Serve warm with vegetable rice.

Nutrition Values Per Serving: Calories: 558; Fat: 9g; Sodium: 994mg; Carbs: 1g; Fiber: 0.4g; Sugar: 3g; Protein: 16g

Herbed Shrimp

Ingredients for Serving: 3

1 lb. shrimp, peeled and deveined.

4 tbsp. salted butter, melted

2 tbsp. chicken broth.

1 tbsp. fresh lemon juice

1 tbsp. garlic, minced.

1 tbsp. fresh chives, chopped.

2 tbsp. fresh basil, chopped.

2 tsp. red pepper flakes, crushed.

Directions and Ready in About: 22-Minutes.

- In a 7-inch round baking pan, place butter, lemon juice, garlic and red pepper flakes and mix well. Press *Power* button of "Ninja Foodi Digital Air Fry Oven" and turn the dial to select the *Air Fry* mode.
- Press *Time/Slice* button and again turn the dial to set the cooking time to 7 minutes. Now, push *Temp/Darkness* button and rotate the dial to set the temperature at 325 Degrees °F or (163 Degrees °C).
- Press *Start/Pause* button to start your Air Fry Oven. When the unit beeps to show that it is preheated, open the oven door and place the pan over wire rack.
- Insert the wire rack in oven. After 2 minutes of cooking in the pan, stir in the shrimp, basil, chives and broth. When cooking time is completed, open the oven door and stir the mixture. Serve hot with the garnishing of scallion.

Nutrition Values Per Serving: Calories: 327; Fat: 18.3g; Sat Fat: 10.6g; Carbs: 4.2g; Fiber: 0.5g; Sugar: 0.3g; Protein: 35.3g

Rum Glazed Shrimp

Ingredients for Serving: 4

1 ½ lbs. shrimp, peeled and deveined.

¼ Captain Morgan Spiced Rum

⅓ cup sweet chili sauce.

¼ cup soy sauce

2 garlic cloves, minced.

1 green onion, thinly sliced

3 tbsp. olive oil

½ tsp. crushed red pepper flakes.

Juice of 1 lime

Directions and Ready in About: 15-Minutes.

- Mix shrimp with all the ingredients in a bowl. Cover and marinate the shrimp for 30 minutes. Spread the glazed shrimp in a sheet pan. Transfer the pan to the "Ninja Foodi Digital Air Fry Oven" and close the door. Select *Bake* mode by rotating the dial.
- Press the *Time/Slice* button and change the value to 5 minutes. Press the *Temp/Darkness* button and change the value to 375 Degrees °F or (190 Degrees °C). Press *Start/Pause* to begin cooking. Serve warm with sautéed asparagus.

Nutrition Values Per Serving: Calories: 378; Fat: 7g; Sodium: 316mg; Carbs: 6.2g; Fiber: 0.3g; Sugar: 0.3g; Protein: 26g

Fish in Yogurt Marinade

Ingredients for Serving: 2

1½ lbs. perch filets.

1 cup plain Greek yogurt

1 tbsp. lemon juice.

1 tbsp. finely minced garlic

3 tbsp. fresh oregano leaves.

1 tsp. ground cumin

¼ tsp. ground allspice.

½ tsp. salt

½ tsp. freshly ground black pepper

Finely grated zest of 1 lemon.

Directions and Ready in About: 25-Minutes.

- Mix lemon zest, yogurt, garlic, cumin, oregano, black pepper, salt and all spices in a shallow pan. Add fish to this marinade, mix well to coat then cover it with a plastic wrap.
- Marinate for 15 minutes in the refrigerator, then uncover. Transfer the fish pan to the "Ninja Foodi Digital Air Fry Oven" and close the door.
- Select *Bake* mode by rotating the dial. Press the *Time/Slice* button and change the value to 10 minutes. Press the *Temp/Darkness* button and change the value to 450 Degrees °F or (232 Degrees °C). Press *Start/Pause* to begin cooking. Serve warm with lemon slices and fried rice.

Nutrition Values Per Serving: Calories: 438; Fat: 21g; Carbs: 7.1g; Fiber: 0.1g; Sugar: 0.4g; Protein: 23g

Spicy Salmon

Ingredients for Serving: 2

2 (6-ounce) (1½-inch thick) salmon fillets.

1 tsp. smoked paprika

1 tsp. onion powder.

1 tsp. garlic powder

2 tsp. olive oil

1 tsp. cayenne pepper.

Salt and ground black pepper, to taste.

Directions and Ready in About: 21-Minutes.

- Add the spices in a bowl and mix well. Drizzle the salmon fillets with oil and then rub with the spice mixture.
- Press *Power* button of "Ninja Foodi Digital Air Fry Oven" and turn the dial to select *Air Fry* mode. Press *Time/Slice* button and again turn the dial to set the cooking time to 11 minutes.
- Now, push *Temp/Darkness* button and rotate the dial to set the temperature at 390 Degrees °F or (199 Degrees °C).
- Press *Start/Pause* button to start your Air Fry Oven. When the unit beeps to show that it is preheated, open the oven door.
- Arrange the salmon fillets into the greased air fry basket and insert in the oven. When cooking time is completed, open the oven door and serve hot with your favorite salad.

Nutrition Values Per Serving: Calories: 280; Fat: 15.5g; Sat Fat: 2.2g; Carbs: 3.1g; Fiber: 0.8g; Sugar: 1g; Protein: 33.6g

Seafood Casserole

Ingredients for Serving: 8

1 lb. large shrimp, peeled and deveined.

1 lb. scallops

8 oz. haddock, skinned and diced.

½ cup Swiss cheese, shredded.

½ cup heavy cream

3 to 4 garlic cloves, minced.

2 tbsp. Parmesan, grated.

Paprika, to taste.

Sea salt and black pepper, to taste.

Directions and Ready in About: 35-Minutes.

- Toss shrimp, scallops and haddock chunks in the sheet pan greased with cooking spray. Drizzle salt, black pepper and minced garlic over the seafood mix.
- Top this seafood with cream, Swiss cheese, paprika and Parmesan cheese. Transfer the dish to the Ninja Digital Air Fryer Oven and close its oven door.
- Select *Bake* mode by rotating the dial. Press the *Time/Slice* button and change the value to 20 minutes.
- Press the *Temp/Darkness* button and change the value to 375 Degrees °F or (190 Degrees °C). Press *Start/Pause* to begin cooking. Serve warm casserole with fresh vegetable salad.

Nutrition Values Per Serving: Calories: 548; Fat: 13g; Sodium: 353mg; Carbs: 31g; Fiber: 0.4g; Sugar: 1g; Protein: 29g

Prawns in Butter Sauce

Ingredients for Serving: 2

½ lb. large prawns, peeled and deveined.

1 large garlic clove, minced.

1 tbsp. butter, melted

1 tsp. fresh lemon zest, grated.

Directions and Ready in About: 21-Minutes.

- Take a bowl, add all the ingredients and toss to coat well. Set aside at room temperature for about 30 minutes. Arrange the prawn mixture into a sheet pan.
- Press *Power* button of "Ninja Foodi Digital Air Fry Oven" and turn the dial to select *Bake* mode. Press *Time/Slice* button and again turn the dial to set the cooking time to 6 minutes.
- Now, push *Temp/Darkness* button and rotate the dial to set the temperature at 450 Degrees °F or (232 Degrees °C).
- Press *Start/Pause* button to start your Air Fry Oven. When the unit beeps to show that it is preheated, open the oven door.
- Arrange the pan over the wire rack and insert in the oven. When cooking time is completed, open the oven door and serve immediately with fresh salad.

Nutrition Values Per Serving: Calories: 189; Fat: 7.7g; Sat Fat: 4.2g; Carbs: 2.4g; Fiber: 0.1g; Sugar: 0.1g; Protein: 26g

Saucy Cod

Ingredients for Serving: 2

2 (7-ounce) cod fillets.

5 little squares rock sugar

2 scallions (green part), sliced.

1 cup water

¼ cup fresh cilantro, chopped.

5 ginger slices

5 tbsp. light soy sauce.

3 tbsp. olive oil

1 tsp. dark soy sauce.

¼ tsp. sesame oil

Salt and ground black pepper, to taste.

Directions and Ready in About: 30-Minutes.

- Season each cod fillet evenly with salt and black pepper and drizzle with sesame oil. Set aside at room temperature for about 15-20 minutes.
- Press *Power* button of "Ninja Foodi Digital Air Fry Oven" and turn the dial to select *Air Fry* mode. Press *Time/Slice* button and again turn the dial to set the cooking time to 12 minutes.
- Now, push *Temp/Darkness* button and rotate the dial to set the temperature at 355 Degrees °F or (179 Degrees °C).
- Press *Start/Pause* button to start your Air Fry Oven. When the unit beeps to show that it is preheated, open the oven door.
- Arrange the cod fillets into the greased air fry basket and insert in the oven. Meanwhile, in a small pan, add the water and bring it to a boil.
- Add the rock sugar and both soy sauces and cook until sugar is dissolved, stirring continuously. Remove from

the heat and set aside. Remove the cod fillets from oven and transfer onto serving plates.

- Top each fillet with scallion and cilantro. In a small frying pan, heat the olive oil over medium heat and sauté the ginger slices for about 2-3 minutes.
- Remove the frying pan from heat and discard the ginger slices. When cooking time is completed, open the oven door and transfer the cod fillets onto serving plates.
- Carefully pour the hot oil evenly over cod fillets. Top with the sauce mixture and serve with boiled rice.

Nutrition Values Per Serving: Calories: 380; Fat: 23.4g; Sat Fat: 3.1g; Carbs: 5g; Fiber: 0.8g; Sugar: 1.1g; Protein: 38.3g

Scallops with Capers Sauce

Ingredients for Serving: 2

10 (1-ounce) sea scallops, cleaned and patted very dry	¼ cup extra-virgin olive oil
	½ tsp. garlic, chopped finely.
2 tbsp. fresh parsley, chopped finely.	2 tsp. capers, chopped finely.
1 tsp. fresh lemon zest, finely grated	Salt and ground black pepper, to taste.

Directions and Ready in About: 16-Minutes.

- Season each scallop evenly with salt and black pepper. Press *Power* button of "Ninja Foodi Digital Air Fry Oven" and turn the dial to select *Air Fry* mode. Press *Time/Slice* button and again turn the dial to set the cooking time to 6 minutes.
- Now, push *Temp/Darkness* button and rotate the dial to set the temperature at 400 Degrees °F or (204 Degrees °C).
- Press *Start/Pause* button to start your Air Fry Oven. When the unit beeps to show that it is preheated, open the oven door and grease the air fry basket.
- Place the scallops into the prepared air fry basket and insert in the oven. Meanwhile, for the sauce: in a bowl, mix the remaining ingredients.
- When cooking time is completed, open the oven door and transfer the scallops onto serving plates. Top with the sauce and serve immediately with a garnishing of fresh herbs.

Nutrition Values Per Serving: Calories: 344; Fat: 26.3g; Sat Fat: 3.7g; Carbs: 4.2g; Fiber: 0.3g; Sugar: 0.1g; Protein: 24g

Spicy Bay Scallops

Ingredients for Serving: 4

1 lb. bay scallops rinsed and patted dry.	⅛ tsp. cayenne red pepper
¼ tsp. ground black pepper	1 tsp. garlic powder
2 tsp. smoked paprika.	2 tsp. chili powder.
2 tsp. olive oil	

Directions and Ready in About: 23-Minutes.

- Scallops with paprika, chili powder, olive oil, garlic powder, black pepper and red pepper in a bowl.

- Place the scallops in the air fry basket. Transfer the basket to the "Ninja Foodi Digital Air Fry Oven" and close the door.
- Select *Air Fry* mode by rotating the dial. Press the *Time/Slice* button and change the value to 8 minutes.
- Press the *Temp/Darkness* button and change the value to 400 Degrees °F or (204 Degrees °C). Press *Start/Pause* to begin cooking. Serve the scallops with crispy onion rings on the side.

Nutrition Values Per Serving: Calories: 476; Fat: 17g; Sodium: 1127mg; Carbs: 4g; Fiber: 1g; Sugar: 3g; Protein: 29g

Cod Burgers

Ingredients for Serving: 4

½ lb. cod fillets.	1 tbsp. fresh parsley, chopped.
½ egg	
1 small scallion, chopped finely.	½ tsp. fresh lime zest, grated finely.
3 tbsp. coconut, grated and divided	½ tsp. red chili paste
	Salt, to taste.
½ tbsp. fresh lime juice	

Directions and Ready in About: 22-Minutes.

- In a food processor, add cod filets, lime zest, egg, chili paste, salt and lime juice and pulse until smooth. Transfer the cod mixture into a bowl.
- Add 1½ tbsp. coconut, scallion and parsley and mix until well combined. Make 4 equal-sized patties from the mixture.
- In a shallow dish, place the remaining coconut. Coat the patties in coconut evenly.
- Press *Power* button of "Ninja Foodi Digital Air Fry Oven" and turn the dial to select *Air Fry* mode. Press *Time/Slice* button and again turn the dial to set the cooking time to 7 minutes.
- Now, push *Temp/Darkness* button and rotate the dial to set the temperature at 375 Degrees °F or (190 Degrees °C).
- Press *Start/Pause* button to start your Air Fry Oven. When the unit beeps to show that it is preheated, open the oven door.
- Arrange the patties into the greased air fry basket and insert in the oven. When cooking time is completed, open the oven door and serve hot alongside with the dipping sauce.

Nutrition Values Per Serving: Calories: 70; Fat: 2.4g; Sat Fat: 1.3g; Carbs: 1.1g; Fiber: 0.4g; Sugar: 0.5g; Protein: 11g

Parmesan Flounder

Ingredients for Serving: 4

4 fillets flounder.	Juice and zest of 1 lemon
¼ cup bread crumbs	Kosher salt, to taste.
¼ cup olive oil.	Freshly ground black pepper.
½ cup Parmesan, grated.	
4 garlic cloves, minced.	

Directions and Ready in About: 35-Minutes.

- Mix parmesan, breadcrumbs and all the ingredients in a bowl and coat the flounder well. Place the fish in a sheet pan. Transfer the fish to the "Ninja Foodi Digital Air Fry Oven" and close the door.
- Select *Bake* mode by rotating the dial. Press the *Time/Slice* button and change the value to 20 minutes. Press the *Temp/Darkness* button and change the value to 425 Degrees °F or (218 Degrees °C). Press *Start/Pause* to begin cooking. Serve warm with fresh greens and yogurt dip.

Nutrition Values Per Serving: Calories: 351; Fat: 4g; Sodium: 236mg; Carbs: 9.1g; Fiber: 0.3g; Sugar: 0.1g; Protein: 36g

Beer Battered Fish

Ingredients for Serving: 4

2 lbs. cod, cut into 12 pieces.	freshly ground black pepper.
1 (12-ounce) bottle lager	vegetable oil for frying
1 large egg, beaten.	lemon wedges, for serving
1 ½ cups all-purpose flour	kosher salt, to taste.
½ tsp. Old Bay seasoning	

Directions and Ready in About: 30-Minutes.

- Mix flour with old bay, salt, egg and beer in a bowl. Rub the cod with black pepper and salt. Coat the codfish with the beer batter and place it in the air fry basket.
- Transfer the basket to the "Ninja Foodi Digital Air Fry Oven" and close the door. Select *Air Fry* mode by rotating the dial.
- Press the *Time/Slice* button and change the value to 15 minutes. Press the *Temp/Darkness* button and change the value to 350 Degrees °F or (176 Degrees °C).
- Press *Start/Pause* to begin cooking. Serve warm with potato fries and tomato ketchup.

Nutrition Values Per Serving: Calories: 428; Fat: 17g; Sodium: 723mg; Carbs: 21g; Fiber: 2.5g; Sugar: 2g; Protein: 43g

Buttered Crab Shells

Ingredients for Serving: 4

4 soft crab shells, cleaned	2 tbsp. butter, melted
2 cups panko breadcrumb	2 tsp. seafood seasoning
1 cup buttermilk	1½ tsp. lemon zest, grated.
3 eggs	

Directions and Ready in About: 35-Minutes.

- Take a shallow bowl, place the buttermilk. In a second bowl, whisk the eggs.
- In a third bowl, mix together the breadcrumbs, seafood seasoning and lemon zest. Soak the crab shells into the buttermilk for about 10 minutes.
- Now, dip the crab shells into beaten eggs and then, coat with the breadcrumb mixture.
- Press *Power* button of "Ninja Foodi Digital Air Fry Oven" and turn the dial to select *Air Fry* mode. Press

Time/Slice button and again turn the dial to set the cooking time to 10 minutes.

- Now, push *Temp/Darkness* button and rotate the dial to set the temperature at 375 Degrees °F or (190 Degrees °C).
- Press *Start/Pause* button to start your Air Fry Oven. When the unit beeps to show that it is preheated, open the oven door and grease the air fry basket.
- Place the crab shells into the prepared air fry basket and insert in the oven. When cooking time is completed, open the oven door and transfer the crab shells onto serving plates.
- Drizzle crab shells with the melted butter and serve immediately alongside with the lemon slices.

Nutrition Values Per Serving: Calories: 549; Fat: 17.3g; Sat Fat: 7g; Carbs: 11.5g; Fiber: 0.3g; Sugar: 3.3g; Protein: 53.5g

Lobster Tail Casserole

Ingredients for Serving: 6

1 lb. salmon fillets, cut into 8 equal pieces.	¼ cup white wine
	¼ cup lemon juice
16 large prawns, peeled and deveined	⅓ cup butter
8 East Coast lobster tails split in half.	2 tbsp. chopped fresh tarragon.
16 large sea scallops	½ tsp. paprika
2 medium garlic cloves, minced.	¼ tsp. ground cayenne pepper.

Directions and Ready in About: 31-Minutes.

- Whisk butter with lemon juice, wine, garlic, tarragon, paprika, salt and cayenne pepper in a small saucepan.
- Stir cook this mixture over medium heat for 1 minute. Toss scallops, salmon fillet and prawns in the Ninja baking dish and pour the butter mixture on top.
- Transfer the dish to the "Ninja Foodi Digital Air Fry Oven" and close the door. Select *Bake* mode by rotating the dial.
- Press the *Time/Slice* button and change the value to 15 minutes. Press the *Temp/Darkness* button and change the value to 450 Degrees °F or (232 Degrees °C). Press *Start/Pause* to begin cooking. Serve warm with fresh greens and chili sauce on the side.

Nutrition Values Per Serving: Calories: 457; Fat: 19g; Carbs: 9g; Fiber: 1.8g; Sugar: 1.2g; Protein: 32.5g

Crab Cakes

Ingredients for Serving: 4

¼ cup red bell pepper, seeded and chopped finely.	2 tbsp. mayonnaise
	2 tbsp. breadcrumbs.
8 oz. lump crabmeat, drained	1 tbsp. Dijon mustard
2 scallions, chopped finely.	1 tsp. old bay seasoning.

Directions and Ready in About: 25-Minutes.

- Take a large bowl, add all the ingredients except crabmeat and mix until well combined. Gently fold in the crabmeat.
- Make 4 equal-sized patties from the mixture. Arrange the patties onto the lightly greased sheet pan.
- Press *Power* button of "Ninja Foodi Digital Air Fry Oven" and turn the dial to select the *Air Fry* mode. Press *Time/Slice* button and again turn the dial to set the cooking time to 10 minutes.
- Now, push *Temp/Darkness* button and rotate the dial to set the temperature at 370 Degrees °F or (187 Degrees °C).
- Press *Start/Pause* button to start your Air Fry Oven. When the unit beeps to show that it is preheated, open the oven door and insert the sheet pan in oven.
- When cooking time is completed, open the oven door and serve hot alongside with the fresh salad.

Nutrition Values Per Serving: Calories: 91; Fat: 7.4g; Sat Fat: 0.4g; Carbs: 6.4g; Fiber: 0.6g; Sugar: 1.3g; Protein: 9.1g

Asparagus Salmon and Parcel

Ingredients for Serving: 2

6 asparagus stalks.	1 tsp. oil
2 (4-ounce) salmon fillets	Salt and ground black pepper, to taste.
¼ cup champagne.	
¼ cup white sauce	

Directions and Ready in About: 28-Minutes.

- Take a bowl, mix together all the ingredients. Divide the salmon mixture over 2 pieces of foil evenly. Seal the foil around the salmon mixture to form the packet.
- Press *Power* button of "Ninja Foodi Digital Air Fry Oven" and turn the dial to select *Air Fry* mode. Press *Time/Slice* button and again turn the dial to set the cooking time to 13 minutes.
- Now, push *Temp/Darkness* button and rotate the dial to set the temperature at 355 Degrees °F or (179 Degrees °C).
- Press *Start/Pause* button to start your Air Fry Oven. When the unit beeps to show that it is preheated, open the oven door.
- Arrange the salmon parcels into the air fry basket and insert in the oven. When cooking time is completed, open the oven door and serve hot with the garnishing of fresh herbs.

Nutrition Values Per Serving: Calories: 243; Fat: 12.7g; Sat Fat: 2.2g; Carbs: 9.4g; Fiber: 1.8g; Sugar: 6g; Protein: 25g

Baked Sardines with Garlic and Oregano

Ingredients for Serving: 4

2 lbs. fresh sardines.	½ cup water
½ cup olive oil	2 tbsp. Greek oregano.
½ cup freshly squeezed lemon juice.	Salt and black pepper to taste
6 cloves garlic, thinly sliced	

Directions and Ready in About: 1 hr.

- Mix salt, black pepper, oregano, garlic, olive oil, lemon juice and water in a baking pan. Spread the sardines in the marinade and rub well.
- Leave the sardines for 10 minutes to marinate. Transfer the pan to the "Ninja Foodi Digital Air Fry Oven" and close the door.
- Select *Air Fry* mode by rotating the dial. Press the *Time/Slice* button and change the value to 45 minutes.
- Press the *Temp/Darkness* button and change the value to 355 Degrees °F or (179 Degrees °C). Press *Start/Pause* to begin cooking. Serve warm with crispy bread and sautéed veggies.

Nutrition Values Per Serving: Calories: 392; Fat: 16g; Carbs: 3.9g; Fiber: 0.9g; Sugar: 0.6g; Protein: 48g

Scallops with Spinach

Ingredients for Serving: 2

1 (12-ounce) package frozen spinach, thawed and drained	8 jumbo sea scallops.
	1 tbsp. tomato paste
¾ cup heavy whipping cream	1 tsp. garlic, minced.
	Olive oil cooking spray
1 tbsp. fresh basil, chopped.	Salt and ground black pepper, to taste.

Directions and Ready in About: 25-Minutes.

- Take a bowl, place the cream, tomato paste, garlic, basil, salt and black pepper and mix well. Spray each scallop evenly with cooking spray and then, sprinkle with a little salt and black pepper.
- In the bottom of a baking pan, place the spinach. Arrange scallops on top of the spinach in a single layer and top with the cream mixture evenly.
- Press *Power* button of "Ninja Foodi Digital Air Fry Oven" and turn the dial to select *Air Fry* mode. Press *Time/Slice* button and again turn the dial to set the cooking time to 10 minutes.
- Now, push *Temp/Darkness* button and rotate the dial to set the temperature at 350 Degrees °F or (176 Degrees °C).
- Press *Start/Pause* button to start your Air Fry Oven. When the unit beeps to show that it is preheated, open the oven door.
- Place the pan into the prepared air fry basket and insert in the oven. When cooking time is completed, open the oven door and serve hot with crusty bread.

Nutrition Values Per Serving: Calories: 309; Fat: 18.8g; Sat Fat: 10.6g; Carbs: 12.3g; Fiber: 4.1g; Sugar: 1.7g; Protein: 26.4g

Fish Newburg with Haddock

Ingredients for Serving: 4

1 ½ lbs. haddock fillets.	3 tbsp. dry sherry
¾ cup heavy cream	1 tbsp and 2 tsp. flour.
4 pastry shells.	¼ tsp. sweet paprika
2 large egg yolks	¼ tsp. ground nutmeg.

| ½ cup milk | Dash cayenne pepper |
| 4 tbsp. butter. | Salt and freshly ground black pepper. |

Directions and Ready in About: 44-Minutes.

- Rub haddock with black pepper and salt, then place in a sheet pan. Place the spiced haddock in the pastry shell and close it like a colzone.
- Drizzle 1 tbsp. of melted butter on top. Transfer the pan to the "Ninja Foodi Digital Air Fry Oven" and close the door. Select *Bake* mode by rotating the dial.
- Press the *Time/Slice* button and change the value to 25 minutes. Press the *Temp/Darkness* button and change the value to 350 Degrees °F or (176 Degrees °C).
- Press *Start/Pause* to begin cooking. Meanwhile, melt 3 tbsp. of butter in a suitable saucepan over low heat.
- Stir in nutmeg, cayenne, paprika and salt, then mix well. Add flour to the spice butter and whisk well to avoid lumps. Cook for 2 minutes, then add milk and cream. Mix well and cook until thickens.
- Beat egg yolks with sherry in a bowl and stir in a ladle of cream mixture. Mix well and return the mixture to the saucepan.
- Cook the mixture on low heat for 2 minutes. Add the baked wrapped haddock to the sauce and cook until warm. Serve warm with fried rice.

Nutrition Values Per Serving: Calories: 421; Fat: 7.4g; Sodium: 356mg; Carbs: 9.3g; Fiber: 2.4g; Sugar: 5g; Protein: 37.2g

Spiced Shrimp

Ingredients for Serving: 3

1 lb. tiger shrimp.	½ tsp. cayenne pepper
3 tbsp. olive oil	1 tsp. old bay seasoning.
½ tsp. smoked paprika.	Salt, to taste.

Directions and Ready in About: 20-Minutes.

- Take a large bowl, add all the ingredients and stir to combine.
- Press *Power* button of "Ninja Foodi Digital Air Fry Oven" and turn the dial to select *Air Fry* mode. Press *Time/Slice* button and again turn the dial to set the cooking time to 5 minutes.
- Now, push *Temp/Darkness* button and rotate the dial to set the temperature at 390 Degrees °F or (199 Degrees °C).
- Press *Start/Pause* button to start your Air Fry Oven. When the unit beeps to show that it is preheated, open the oven door.
- Arrange the shrimp into the greased air fry basket and insert in the oven. When cooking time is completed, open the oven door and serve hot with fresh greens.

Nutrition Values Per Serving: Calories: 272; Fat: 15.7g; Sat Fat: 2.5g; Carbs: 0.4g; Fiber: 0.2g; Sugar: 0.1g; Protein: 31.7g

Vegetables and Sides Dishes

Cauliflower and Broccoli Roast

Ingredients for Serving: 4

½ lb. cauliflower, florets.

½ lb. broccoli, florets

⅓ cup water.

1 tbsp. olive oil

Salt, to taste.

Black pepper, to taste.

Directions and Ready in About: 25-Minutes.

- Toss all the veggies with seasoning in a large bowl. Spread these vegetables in the air fry basket.
- Transfer the basket to the "Ninja Foodi Digital Air Fry Oven" and close the door. Select *Air Fry* mode by rotating the dial.
- Press the *Time/Slice* button and change the value to 10 minutes. Press the *Temp/Darkness* button and change the value to 400 Degrees °F or (204 Degrees °C). Press *Start/Pause* to begin cooking. Serve warm with white rice.

Nutrition Values Per Serving: Calories: 318; Fat: 15.7g; Sodium: 124mg; Carbs: 7g; Fiber: 0.1g; Sugar: 0.3g; Protein: 4.9g

Spicy and Sweet Parsnips

Ingredients for Serving: 5

1½ lbs. parsnip, peeled and cut into 1-inch chunks.

1 tbsp. dried parsley flakes, crushed

1 tbsp. butter, melted.

2 tbsp. honey

¼ tsp. red pepper flakes, crushed

Salt and ground black pepper, to taste.

- Directions and Ready in About: 1 hr.
- Take a large bowl, mix together the parsnips and butter. Press *Power* button of "Ninja Foodi Digital Air Fry Oven" and turn the dial to select *Air Fry* mode.
- Press *Time/Slice* button and again turn the dial to set the cooking time to 44 minutes. Now, push *Temp/Darkness* button and rotate the dial to set the temperature at 355 Degrees °F or (179 Degrees °C).
- Press *Start/Pause* button to start your Air Fry Oven. When the unit beeps to show that it is preheated, open the oven door.
- Arrange the parsnip chunks into the greased air fry basket and insert in the oven. Meanwhile, in another large bowl, mix together the remaining ingredients.
- After 40 minutes of cooking, press *Start/Pause* button to pause the unit. Transfer the parsnip chunks into the bowl of honey mixture and toss to coat well.
- Again, arrange the parsnip chunks into the air fry basket and insert in the oven. When cooking time is completed, open the oven door and serve hot with garlic bread.

Nutrition Values Per Serving: Calories: 149; Fat: 2.7g; Sat Fat: 1.5g; Carbs: 31.5g; Fiber: 6.7g; Sugar: 13.5g; Protein: 1.7g

Spicy Potato

Ingredients for Serving: 4

6 russet potatoes, peeled and cubed.

½ of onion, chopped.

1 garlic clove, minced.

2 cups water

1 jalapeño pepper, chopped.

½ tbsp. extra-virgin olive oil

1 tbsp. fresh rosemary, chopped.

¼ tsp. red chili powder

½ tsp. garam masala powder

¼ tsp. ground cumin

Salt and ground black pepper, to taste.

Directions and Ready in About: 40-Minutes.

- Take a large bowl, add the water and potatoes and set aside for about 30 minutes. Drain well and pat dry with the paper towels.
- Take a bowl, add the potatoes and oil and toss to coat well. Press *Power* button of "Ninja Foodi Digital Air Fry Oven" and turn the dial to select *Air Fry* mode. Press *Time/Slice* button and again turn the dial to set the cooking time to 5 minutes.
- Now, push *Temp/Darkness* button and rotate the dial to set the temperature at 330 Degrees °F or (166 Degrees °C).
- Press *Start/Pause* button to start your Air Fry Oven. When the unit beeps to show that it is preheated, open the oven door.
- Arrange the potato cubes in air fry basket and insert in the oven. Remove from oven and transfer the potatoes into a bowl.
- Add the remaining ingredients and toss to coat well. Press *Power* button of "Ninja Foodi Digital Air Fry Oven" and turn the dial to select *Air Fry* mode. Press *Time/Slice* button and again turn the dial to set the cooking time to 20 minutes.
- Now, push *Temp/Darkness* button and rotate the dial to set the temperature at 390 Degrees °F or (199 Degrees °C).
- Press *Start/Pause* button to start your Air Fry Oven. When the unit beeps to show that it is preheated, open the oven door.
- Arrange the potato mixture in air fry basket and insert in the oven. When cooking time is completed, open the oven door and serve hot with plain bread.

Nutrition Values Per Serving: Calories: 274; Fat: 2.3g; Sat Fat: 0.4g; Carbs: 52.6g; Fiber: 8.5g; Sugar: 4.4g; Protein: 5.7g

Quinoa Burgers

Ingredients for Serving: 4

½ cup cooked and cooled quinoa.

¼ cup feta cheese, crumbled

¼ cup white onion, minced.

2 eggs, lightly beaten

1 cup rolled oats.

Olive oil cooking spray

Salt and ground black pepper, to taste.

Directions and Ready in About: 20-Minutes.

- Take a large bowl, add all ingredients and mix until well combined. Make 4 equal-sized patties from the mixture.
- Lightly spray the patties with cooking spray. Press *Power* button of "Ninja Foodi Digital Air Fry Oven" and turn the dial to select *Air Fry* mode.
- Press *Time/Slice* button and again turn the dial to set the cooking time to 10 minutes. Now, push *Temp/Darkness* button and rotate the dial to set the temperature at 400 Degrees °F or (204 Degrees °C).
- Press *Start/Pause* button to start your Air Fry Oven. When the unit beeps to show that it is preheated, open the oven door.
- Arrange the patties into the greased air fry basket and insert in the oven. Flip the patties once halfway through. When cooking time is completed, open the oven door and transfer the patties onto a platter. Serve warm with green sauce.

Nutrition Values Per Serving: Calories: 215; Fat: 6.6g; Sat Fat: 2.5g; Carbs: 28.7g; Fiber: 3.7g; Sugar: 1.1g; Protein: 9.9g

Wine Braised Mushrooms

Ingredients for Serving: 6

2 lbs. fresh mushrooms, quartered.

2 tbsp. white wine

1 tbsp. butter.

2 tsp. Herbs de Provence

½ tsp. garlic powder.

Directions and Ready in About: 42-Minutes.

- In a frying pan, mix together the butter, Herbs de Provence and garlic powder over medium-low heat and stir fry for about 2 minutes.
- Stir in the mushrooms and remove from the heat. Transfer the mushroom mixture into a sheet pan.
- Press *Power* button of "Ninja Foodi Digital Air Fry Oven" and turn the dial to select *Air Fry* mode. Press *Time/Slice* button and again turn the dial to set the cooking time to 30 minutes.
- Now, push *Temp/Darkness* button and rotate the dial to set the temperature at 320 Degrees °F or (160 Degrees °C).
- Press *Start/Pause* button to start your Air Fry Oven. When the unit beeps to show that it is preheated, open the oven door.
- Arrange the pan over the wire rack and insert in the oven. After 25 minutes of cooking, stir the wine into mushroom mixture. When cooking time is completed, open the oven door and serve hot with a garnishing of fresh herbs.

Nutrition Values Per Serving: Calories: 54; Fat: 2.4g; Sat Fat: 1.2g; Carbs: 5.3g; Fiber: 1.5g; Sugar: 2.7g; Protein: 4.8g

Tofu with Broccoli

Ingredients for Serving: 2

8 oz. block firm tofu, pressed and cubed.

1 small head broccoli, cut into florets

1 tbsp. nutritional yeast.

1 tbsp. canola oil

¼ tsp. dried parsley

Salt and ground black pepper, to taste.

Directions and Ready in About: 30-Minutes.

- Take a bowl, mix together the tofu, broccoli and the remaining ingredients. Press *Power* button of "Ninja Foodi Digital Air Fry Oven" and turn the dial to select *Air Fry* mode.
- Press *Time/Slice* button and again turn the dial to set the cooking time to 15 minutes. Now, push *Temp/Darkness* button and rotate the dial to set the temperature at 390 Degrees °F or (199 Degrees °C).
- Press *Start/Pause* button to start your Air Fry Oven. When the unit beeps to show that it is preheated, open the oven door.
- Arrange the tofu mixture into the greased air fry basket and insert in the oven. Flip the tofu mixture once halfway through.
- When cooking time is completed, open the oven door and serve hot with the garnishing of sesame seeds.

Nutrition Values Per Serving: Calories: 206; Fat: 13.1g; Sat Fat: 1.6g; Carbs: 12.1g; Fiber: 5.4g; Sugar: 2.6g; Protein: 15g

Caramelized Baby Carrots

Ingredients for Serving: 4

1 lb. bag baby carrots.

½ cup butter, melted

½ cup brown sugar.

Directions and Ready in About: 25-Minutes.

- Take a bowl, mix together the butter, brown sugar and carrots. Press *Power* button of "Ninja Foodi Digital Air Fry Oven" and turn the dial to select *Air Fry* mode.
- Press *Time/Slice* button and again turn the dial to set the cooking time to 15 minutes. Now, push *Temp/Darkness* button and rotate the dial to set the temperature at 400 Degrees °F or (204 Degrees °C).
- Press *Start/Pause* button to start your Air Fry Oven. When the unit beeps to show that it is preheated, open the oven door.
- Arrange the carrots in a greased air fry basket and insert in the oven. When cooking time is completed, open the oven door and serve warm with favorite greens.

Nutrition Values Per Serving: Calories: 312; Fat: 23.2g; Sat Fat: 14.5g; Carbs: 27.1g; Fiber: 3.3g; Sugar: 23g; Protein: 1g

Broccoli with Cauliflower

Ingredients for Serving: 4

1½ cups cauliflower, cut into 1-inch pieces.

1 tbsp. olive oil.

1½ cups broccoli, cut into 1-inch pieces

Salt, to taste.

Directions and Ready in About: 35-Minutes.

- Take a bowl, add the vegetables, oil and salt and toss to coat well. Press *Power* button of "Ninja Foodi Digital Air Fry Oven" and turn the dial to select *Air Fry* mode.

- Press *Time/Slice* button and again turn the dial to set the cooking time to 20 minutes. Now, push *Temp/Darkness* button and rotate the dial to set the temperature at 375 Degrees °F or (190 Degrees °C).
- Press *Start/Pause* button to start your Air Fry Oven. When the unit beeps to show that it is preheated, open the oven door.
- Arrange the veggie mixture into the greased air fry basket and insert in the oven. When cooking time is completed, open the oven door and serve hot with the drizzling of lemon juice.

Nutrition Values Per Serving: Calories: 51; Fat: 3.7g; Sat Fat: 0.5g; Carbs: 4.3g; Fiber: 1.8g; Sugar: 1.5g; Protein: 1.7g

Herbed Bell Peppers

Ingredients for Serving: 4

1½ lbs. mixed bell peppers, seeded and sliced.	1 small onion, sliced.
2 tbsp. butter, melted	½ tsp. dried thyme, crushed.
½ tsp. dried savory, crushed	Salt and ground black pepper, to taste.

Directions and Ready in About: 18-Minutes.

- Take a bowl, add the bell peppers, onion, herbs, salt and black pepper and toss to coat well. Press *Power* button of "Ninja Foodi Digital Air Fry Oven" and turn the dial to select *Air Fry* mode.
- Press *Time/Slice* button and again turn the dial to set the cooking time to 8 minutes. Now, push *Temp/Darkness* button and rotate the dial to set the temperature at 360 Degrees °F or (182 Degrees °C).
- Press *Start/Pause* button to start your Air Fry Oven. When the unit beeps to show that it is preheated, open the oven door.
- Arrange the bell peppers into the air fry basket and insert in the oven. When cooking time is completed, open the oven door and transfer the bell peppers into a bowl. Drizzle with butter and serve immediately with boiled rice.

Nutrition Values Per Serving: Calories: 73; Fat: 5.9g; Sat Fat: 3.7g; Carbs: 5.2g; Fiber: 1.1g; Sugar: 3g; Protein: 0.7g

Sweet Potato Casserole

Ingredients for Serving: 6

3 cups sweet potatoes, mashed and cooled.	⅓ cup flour
¾ cup butter, melted	1 ½ cups brown sugar, packed.
4 oz. pecans, chopped.	½ cup milk
2 large eggs, beaten	1 tsp. vanilla extract.

Directions and Ready in About: 50-Minutes.

- Mix the sweet potato mash with vanilla extract, milk, eggs, 1 cup of brown sugar and ½ cup of melted butter in a large bowl.
- Spread this sweet potato mixture in a casserole dish. Now, whisk remaining sugar and butter with flour in a separate bowl.

- Fold in pecan, then top the sweet potatoes mixed with this pecan mixture. Transfer the dish to the "Ninja Foodi Digital Air Fry Oven" and close the door.
- Select *Bake* mode by rotating the dial. Press the *Time/Slice* button and change the value to 35 minutes. Press the *Temp/Darkness* button and change the value to 350 Degrees °F or (176 Degrees °C).
- Press *Start/Pause* to begin cooking. Slice and serve with roasted pecans.

Nutrition Values Per Serving: Calories: 353; Fat: 3g; Sodium: 510mg; Carbs: 32g; Fiber: 3g; Sugar: 4g; Protein: 4g

Blue Cheese Soufflés

Ingredients for Serving: 4

10 oz. semi-skimmed milk.	1 oz. plain flour.
3 oz. blue murder cheese	1 pinch English mustard powder
2 oz. unsalted butter.	
4 medium eggs, separated	1 pinch cayenne pepper
1 oz. breadcrumbs	1 fresh thyme sprig, chopped.

Directions and Ready in About: 32-Minutes.

- Grease four ramekins with butter and sprinkle with breadcrumbs. Melt butter in a suitable saucepan, stir in flour, cayenne and mustard powder.
- Then mix well and cook for 1 minute, then slowly pour in the milk. Mix well until smooth, then boil the sauce. Cook for 2 minutes.
- Stir in cheese and mix well until melted. Add black pepper, salt and egg yolks.
- Beat egg whites in a bowl with a mixer until they make stiff peaks. Add egg whites to the cheese sauce, then mix well.
- Divide the mixture into the ramekins and transfer to the Ninja Digital Air Fry Oven, then close its door.
- Select the *Bake* mode by rotating the dial. Press the *Time/Slice* button and change the value to 14 minutes.
- Press the *Temp/Darkness* button and change the value to 350 Degrees °F or (176 Degrees °C). Press *Start/Pause* to begin cooking. Serve warm with sautéed asparagus and toasted bread slices.

Nutrition Values Per Serving: Calories: 236; Fat: 10g; Sodium: 249mg; Carbs: 8g; Fiber: 2g; Sugar: 3g; Protein: 4g

Vegan Cakes

Ingredients for Serving: 8

1 (398 grams) can heart of palm, drained.	4 sheets nori
¾ cup canned artichoke hearts, drained	1½-inch knob of fresh ginger
4 potatoes, diced and boiled.	1 tbsp. tamari
	4 tbsp. red curry paste.
1 lime, zest and juice	Black pepper, to taste.
1 bunch green onions.	Salt, to taste.

Directions and Ready in About: 30-Minutes.

- Add potatoes, green onions, lime zest, juice and the rest of the ingredients to a food processor. Press the pulse button and blend until smooth.
- Make 8 small patties out of this mixture. Place the patties in the air fry basket. Transfer the basket to the "Ninja Foodi Digital Air Fry Oven" and close the door.
- Select *Air Fry* mode by rotating the dial. Press the *Time/Slice* button and change the value to 15 minutes.
- Press the *Temp/Darkness* button and change the value to 400 Degrees °F or (204 Degrees °C). Press *Start/Pause* to begin cooking. Serve warm with roasted asparagus.

Nutrition Values Per Serving: Calories: 324; Fat: 5g; Sodium: 432mg; Carbs: 13.1g; Fiber: 0.3g; Sugar: 1g; Protein: 5.7g

Tofu in Sweet and Sour Sauce

Ingredients for Serving: 4

For Tofu:

1 (14-ounce) block firm tofu, pressed and cubed.

½ cup arrowroot flour

½ tsp. sesame oil.

For Sauce:

2 large garlic cloves, minced.

2 scallions (green part), chopped.

4 tbsp. low-sodium soy sauce

1 tbsp. agave nectar

1½ tbsp. chili sauce.

1½ tbsp. rice vinegar

1 tsp. fresh ginger, peeled and grated.

Directions and Ready in About: 40-Minutes.

- Take a bowl, mix together the tofu, arrowroot flour and sesame oil. Press *Power* button of "Ninja Foodi Digital Air Fry Oven" and turn the dial to select *Air Fry* mode.
- Press *Time/Slice* button and again turn the dial to set the cooking time to 20 minutes.
- Now, push *Temp/Darkness* button and rotate the dial to set the temperature at 360 Degrees °F or (182 Degrees °C).
- Press *Start/Pause* button to start your Air Fry Oven. When the unit beeps to show that it is preheated, open the oven door.
- Arrange the tofu cubes in greased air fry basket and insert in the oven. Flip the tofu cubes once halfway through.
- Meanwhile, for the sauce: in a bowl, add all the ingredients except scallions and beat until well combined. When cooking time is completed, open the oven door and remove the tofu.
- Transfer the tofu into a skillet with sauce over medium heat and cook for about 3 minutes, stirring occasionally. Garnish with scallions and serve hot with plain boiled rice.

Nutrition Values Per Serving: Calories: 115; Fat: 4.8g; Sat Fat: 1g; Carbs: 10.2g; Fiber: 1.7g; Sugar: 5.6g; Protein: 0.1g

Cheesy Green Bean Casserole

Ingredients for Serving: 6

8 oz. mushrooms, sliced.

4 cups green beans, cooked and chopped

¼ cup onion, chopped.

1 ½ cups milk

¼ cup Parmesan cheese, grated.

1 cup French fried onions

1 cup soft breadcrumbs

2 cups cheddar cheese, shredded.

2 tbsp. sour cream

2 tbsp. butter, melted.

3 tbsp. butter

2 tbsp. flour

1 tsp. salt

¼ tsp. ground black pepper

Directions and Ready in About: 50-Minutes.

- Add butter to a suitable saucepan and melt it over medium-low heat. Toss in onion and mushrooms, then sauté until soft.
- Stir in flour, salt and black pepper. Mix well, then slowly pour in the milk. Stir in sour cream, green beans and cheddar cheese, then cook until it thickens.
- Transfer this green bean mixture to a casserole dish and spread it evenly. Toss breadcrumbs with fried onion and butter.
- Top the casserole with this bread crumbs mixture. Transfer the dish to the "Ninja Foodi Digital Air Fry Oven" and close the door.
- Select *Bake* mode by rotating the dial. Press the *Time/Slice* button and change the value to 25 minutes.
- Press the *Temp/Darkness* button and change the value to 350 Degrees °F or (176 Degrees °C). Press *Start/Pause* to begin cooking. Serve with mashed cauliflower.

Nutrition Values Per Serving: Calories: 304; Fat: 31g; Carbs: 21.4g; Fiber: 0.2g; Sugar: 0.3g; Protein: 4.6g

Cheesy Vegetable Bake

Ingredients for Serving: 4

½ cup brown rice, cooked.

5 oz. feta cheese, cubed.

1 onion, julienned

2 good handful cherry tomatoes

1 bell pepper, red, julienned

1 jalapeño, chopped.

1 handful olives, sliced.

1 garlic clove

2 tbsp. parsley, dried

2 tbsp. olive oil

2 tbsp. basil, dried

10 tbsp. water

Directions and Ready in About: 45-Minutes.

- Spread the cheese in a sheet pan and drizzle half of the herbs on top. Toss remaining vegetables with rice and water, spread over the cheese.
- Add remaining herbs on top and spread them evenly. Transfer the pan to the "Ninja Foodi Digital Air Fry Oven" and close the door.

- Select *Bake* mode by rotating the dial. Press the *Temp/Darkness* button and change the value to 350 Degrees °F or (176 Degrees °C).
- Press the *Time/Slice* button and change the value to 30 minutes, then press *Start/Pause* to begin cooking. Serve warm with warmed tortillas, avocado slices, tomato sauce or guacamole.

Nutrition Values Per Serving: Calories: 391; Fat: 2.2g; Carbs: 27g; Fiber: 0.9g; Sugar: 1.4g; Protein: 8.8g

Roasted Vegetables

Ingredients for Serving: 6

2 medium carrots, peeled and sliced.

1 medium broccoli, florets

2 medium bell peppers cored, chopped.

1 cup grape tomatoes

½ red onion, peeled and diced.

2 garlic cloves, minced.

1 small zucchini, ends trimmed, sliced.

1 tbsp. fresh lemon juice

2 tbsp. olive oil

1 ½ tsp. Italian seasoning

Salt and freshly ground black pepper.

Directions and Ready in About: 30-Minutes.

- Toss all the veggies with olive oil, Italian seasoning, salt, black pepper and garlic in a large salad bowl. Spread this broccoli-zucchini mixture in the sheet pan.
- Transfer the pan to the "Ninja Foodi Digital Air Fry Oven" and close the door. Select *Bake* mode by rotating the dial.
- Press the *Time/Slice* button and change the value to 15 minutes. Press the *Temp/Darkness* button and change the value to 400 Degrees °F or (204 Degrees °C).
- Press *Start/Pause* to begin cooking. Serve warm with lemon juice on top with guacamole on the side.

Nutrition Values Per Serving: Calories: 346; Fat: 15g; Carbs: 4.3g; Fiber: 2.4g; Sugar: 1.2g; Protein: 12.4g

Vinegar Green Beans

Ingredients for Serving: 2

¼ cup nutritional yeast.

1 (10-ounce) bag frozen cut green beans

3 tbsp. balsamic vinegar

Salt and ground black pepper, to taste.

Directions and Ready in About: 30-Minutes.

- Take a bowl, add the green beans, nutritional yeast, vinegar, salt and black pepper and toss to coat well. Press *Power* button of "Ninja Foodi Digital Air Fry Oven" and turn the dial to select *Air Fry* mode.
- Press *Time/Slice* button and again turn the dial to set the cooking time to 20 minutes. Now, push *Temp/Darkness* button and rotate the dial to set the temperature at 400 Degrees °F or (204 Degrees °C).
- Press *Start/Pause* button to start your Air Fry Oven. When the unit beeps to show that it is preheated, open the oven door.
- Arrange the green beans into the greased air fry basket and insert in the oven. When cooking time is completed,

open the oven door and serve hot with the garnishing of sesame seeds.

Nutrition Values Per Serving: Calories: 115; Fat: 1.3g; Sat Fat: 0.2g; Carbs: 18.5g; Fiber: 9.3g; Sugar: 1.8g; Protein: 11.3g

Beans and Veggie Burgers

Ingredients for Serving: 4

1 cup fresh spinach, chopped.

1 cup fresh mushrooms, chopped.

1 cup cooked black beans

2 cups boiled potatoes, peeled and mashed.

2 tsp. Chile lime seasoning

Olive oil cooking spray

Directions and Ready in About: 37-Minutes.

- Take a large bowl, add the beans, potatoes, spinach, mushrooms and seasoning and with your hands, mix until well combined.
- Make 4 equal-sized patties from the mixture. Spray the patties with cooking spray evenly.
- Press *Power* button of "Ninja Foodi Digital Air Fry Oven" and turn the dial to select *Air Fry* mode. Press *Time/Slice* button and again turn the dial to set the cooking time to 22 minutes.
- Now, push *Temp/Darkness* button and rotate the dial to set the temperature at 370 Degrees °F or (187 Degrees °C).
- Press *Start/Pause* button to start your Air Fry Oven. When the unit beeps to show that it is preheated, open the oven door.
- Arrange the patties in the greased air fry basket and insert in the oven. Flip the patties once after 12 minutes.
- When cooking time is completed, open the oven door and remove the air fry basket from the oven. Serve with avocado and tomato salad.

Nutrition Values Per Serving: Calories: 113; Fat: 0.4g; Sat Fat: 0g; Carbohydrates:23.1g; Fiber: 6.2g; Sugar: 1.7g; Protein: 6g

Pita Bread Pizza

Ingredients for Serving: 1

½ oz. part-skim mozzarella cheese, shredded.

½ cup fresh baby spinach leaves.

½ of small plum tomato, cut into 4 slices

1 whole-wheat pita bread

½ of garlic clove, sliced. thinly

2 tbsp. marinara sauce.

½ tbsp. Parmigiano-Reggiano cheese, shredded.

Directions and Ready in About: 15-Minutes.

- Arrange the pita bread onto a plate. Spread marinara sauce over 1 side of each pita bread evenly. Top with the spinach leaves, followed by tomato slices, garlic and cheeses.
- Press *Power* button of "Ninja Foodi Digital Air Fry Oven" and turn the dial to select *Air Fry* mode. Press *Time/Slice* button and again turn the dial to set the cooking time to 5 minutes.
- Now, push *Temp/Darkness* button and rotate the dial to set the temperature at 350 Degrees °F or (176 Degrees

°C). Press *Start/Pause* button to start your Air Fry Oven.

- When the unit beeps to show that it is preheated, open the oven door. Arrange the pita bread into the greased air fry basket and insert in the oven.
- When cooking time is completed, open the oven door and transfer the pizza onto a serving plate. Set aside to cool slightly. Serve warm alongside with the greens.

Nutrition Values Per Serving: Calories: 266; Fat: 6.2g; Sat Fat: 2.6g; Carbs: 43.1g; Fiber: 6.5g; Sugar: 4.6g; Protein: 13g

Broccoli Casserole

Ingredients for Serving: 6

20 oz. chopped broccoli.	2 tbsp. butter
10 ½ oz. cream of celery soup	2 tbsp. onion, minced.
2 large eggs, beaten	1 tbsp. Worcestershire sauce
1 cup Cheddar cheese, grated.	1 tsp. seasoned salt
1 cup mayonnaise.	Black pepper, to taste.

Directions and Ready in About: 1 hr.

- Whisk mayonnaise with eggs, condensed soup in a large bowl. Stir in salt, black pepper, Worcestershire sauce and cheddar cheese.
- Spread broccoli and onion in a greased casserole dish. Top the veggies with the mayonnaise mixture. Transfer this broccoli casserole to the "Ninja Foodi Digital Air Fry Oven" and close its oven door.
- Rotate the Ninja Foodi dial to select the *Bake* mode. Press the *Time/Slice* button and again use the dial to set the cooking time to 45 minutes. Now, Press the *Temp/Darkness* button and rotate the dial to set the temperature at 350 Degrees °F or (176 Degrees °C). Slice and serve warm with spaghetti or any other pasta.

Nutrition Values Per Serving: Calories: 341; Fat: 24g; Carbs: 26.4g; Fiber: 1.2g; Sugar: 1g; Protein: 10.3g

Air Fried Tortellini

Ingredients for Serving: 8

1 cup all-purpose flour.	½ tsp. garlic powder.
1 cup Panko breadcrumbs	½ tsp. crushed red pepper flakes
2 large eggs	
1 (9-ounce) package cheese tortellini.	Freshly ground black pepper, to taste.
⅓ cup Parmesan, grated.	Kosher salt, to taste.
1 tsp. dried oregano	

Directions and Ready in About: 25-Minutes.

- Boil tortellini according to salted boiling water according to package's instructions, then drain. Mix panko with garlic powder, black pepper, salt, red pepper flakes, oregano, Parmesan in a small bowl.

- Beat eggs in one bowl and spread flour on a plate. Coat the tortellini with the flour, dip into the eggs and then coat with the panko mixture.
- Spread the tortellini in the air fry basket and spray them with cooking oil. Transfer the basket to the "Ninja Foodi Digital Air Fry Oven" and close the door.
- Select *Air Fry* mode by rotating the dial. Press the *Time/Slice* button and change the value to 10 minutes.
- Press the *Temp/Darkness* button and change the value to 400 Degrees °F or (204 Degrees °C). Press *Start/Pause* to begin cooking. Serve the tortellini with tomato sauce on the side.

Nutrition Values Per Serving: Calories: 151; Fat: 19g; Sodium: 412mg; Carbs: 23g; Fiber: 0.3g; Sugar: 1g; Protein: 3g

Vegetable Casserole

Ingredients for Serving: 6

1 cup breadcrumbs	1 ½ cups carrots, sliced.
8 oz. mushrooms, sliced.	4 tbsp. all-purpose flour
½ cup Parmesan cheese, grated.	7 tbsp. butter
2 cups peas	½ tsp. mustard powder.
2 cups milk	Salt and black pepper, to taste.
1 ½ cups celery, sliced.	

Directions and Ready in About: 57-Minutes.

- Grease and rub a casserole dish with butter and keep it aside. Add carrots, onion and celery to a saucepan, then fill it with water.
- Cover this pot and cook for 10 minutes, then stir in peas. Cook for 4 minutes, then strain the vegetables.
- Now, melt 1 tbsp. of butter in the same saucepan and toss in mushrooms to sauté. Once the mushrooms are soft, transfer them to the vegetables.
- Prepare the sauce by melting 4 tbsp. of butter in a suitable saucepan.
- Stir in mustard and flour, then stir cook for 2 minutes. Gradually pour in the milk and stir cook until thickened, then add salt and black pepper.
- Add vegetables and mushrooms to the flour milk mixture and mix well. Spread this vegetable blend in the casserole dish evenly.
- Toss the breadcrumbs with the remaining butter and spread it on top of vegetables. Top this casserole dish with cheese.
- Transfer the dish to the "Ninja Foodi Digital Air Fry Oven" and close the door. Select *Air Fry* mode by rotating the dial.
- Press the *Time/Slice* button and change the value to 25 minutes. Press the *Temp/Darkness* button and change the value to 350 Degrees °F or (176 Degrees °C).
- Press *Start/Pause* to begin cooking. Serve warm with a tortilla.

Nutrition Values Per Serving: Calories: 338; Fat: 24g; Carbs: 18.3g; Fiber: 2.4g; Sugar: 1.2g; Protein: 5.4g

Veggie Rice

Ingredients for Serving: 2

2 cups cooked white rice.	2 tsp. sesame oil, toasted and divided
1 large egg, lightly beaten	1 tsp. soy sauce
½ cup frozen peas, thawed.	1 tsp. Sriracha sauce.
½ cup frozen carrots, thawed	½ tsp. sesame seeds, toasted
1 tbsp. water	Salt and ground white pepper, to taste.
1 tbsp. vegetable oil.	

Directions and Ready in About: 33-Minutes.

- Take a large bowl, add the rice, vegetable oil, one tsp. of sesame oil, water, salt and white pepper and mix well. Transfer rice mixture into a lightly greased sheet pan.
- Press *Power* button of "Ninja Foodi Digital Air Fry Oven" and turn the dial to select *Air Fry* mode. Press *Time/Slice* button and again turn the dial to set the cooking time to 18 minutes.
- Now, push *Temp/Darkness* button and rotate the dial to set the temperature at 380 Degrees °F or (193 Degrees °C).
- Press *Start/Pause* button to start your Air Fry Oven. When the unit beeps to show that it is preheated, open the oven door. Place the pan over the wire rack and insert in the oven. While cooking, stir the mixture once after 12 minutes. After 12 minutes of cooking, press *Start/Pause* to pause cooking.
- Remove the pan from oven and place the beaten egg over rice. Again, insert the pan in the oven and press *Start/Pause* to resume cooking.
- After 16 minutes of cooking, press *Start/Pause* to pause cooking. Remove the pan from and stir in the peas and carrots.
- Again, insert the pan in the oven and press *Start/Pause* to resume cooking. Meanwhile, in a bowl, mix together the soy sauce, Sriracha sauce, sesame seeds and the remaining sesame oil.
- When cooking time is completed, open the oven door and transfer the rice mixture into a serving bowl. Drizzle with the sauce mixture and serve with yogurt sauce.

Nutrition Values Per Serving: Calories: 443; Fat: 16.4g; Sat Fat: 3.2g; Carbs: 62.3g; Fiber: 3.6g; Sugar: 3.6g; Protein: 10.1g

Brussels Sprouts ratin

Ingredients for Serving: 6

1 lb. Brussels sprouts.	1 cup milk
½ cup fontina cheese, shredded.	1 garlic clove, cut in half
½ cup fine bread crumbs	2 tbsp. all-purpose flour.
1 dash ground nutmeg	3 tbsp. butter, divided.
1 strip of bacon, cooked and crumbled.	2 tbsp. shallots, minced.
Kosher salt, to taste.	Freshly ground black pepper

Directions and Ready in About: 50-Minutes.

- Trim the Brussels sprouts and remove their outer leaves. Slice the sprouts into quarters, then rinse them under cold water.
- Grease a gratin dish with cooking spray and rub it with garlic halves. Boil salted water in a suitable pan, then add Brussels sprouts.
- Cook the sprouts for 3 minutes, then immediately drain. Place a suitable saucepan over medium-low heat and melt 2 tbsp. of butter in it.
- Toss in shallots and sauté until soft, then stir in flour, nutmeg, ½ tsp. of salt and black pepper.
- Stir cook for 2 minutes, then gradually add milk and a half and half cream. Mix well and add bacon along with shredded cheese.
- Fold in Brussels sprouts and transfer this mixture to the casserole dish. Toss breadcrumbs with 1 tbsp. butter and spread over the casserole.
- Transfer the gratin to the "Ninja Foodi Digital Air Fry Oven" and close the door. Select *Bake* mode by rotating the dial.
- Press the *Time/Slice* button and change the value to 25 minutes. Press the *Temp/Darkness* button and change the value to 350 Degrees °F or (176 Degrees °C).
- Press *Start/Pause* to begin cooking. Serve the gratin with mashed potatoes.

Nutrition Values Per Serving: Calories: 378; Fat: 3.8g; Carbs: 33.3g; Fiber: 2.4g; Sugar: 1.2g; Protein: 14g

Soy Sauce Green Beans

Ingredients for Serving: 2

8 oz. fresh green beans, trimmed and cut in half.	1 tbsp. soy sauce
	1 tsp. sesame oil.

Directions and Ready in About: 20-Minutes.

- Take a bowl, mix together the green beans, soy sauce and sesame oil. Press *Power* button of "Ninja Foodi Digital Air Fry Oven" and turn the dial to select *Air Fry* mode.
- Press *Time/Slice* button and again turn the dial to set the cooking time to 10 minutes.
- Now, push *Temp/Darkness* button and rotate the dial to set the temperature at 390 Degrees °F or (199 Degrees °C). Press *Start/Pause* button to start your Air Fry Oven.
- When the unit beeps to show that it is preheated, open the oven door. Arrange the green beans in air fry basket and insert in the oven.
- When cooking time is completed, open the oven door and serve hot with the garnishing of sesame seeds.

Nutrition Values Per Serving: Calories: 62; Fat: 2.6g; Sat Fat: 0.4g; Carbs: 8.8g; Fiber: 4g; Sugar: 1.7g; Protein: 2.6g

Cheesy Kale

Ingredients for Serving: 3

1 lb. fresh kale, tough ribs removed and chopped.

1 cup goat cheese, crumbled

3 tbsp. olive oil.

1 tsp. fresh lemon juice

Salt and ground black pepper, to taste.

Directions and Ready in About: 25-Minutes.

- Take a bowl, add the kale, oil, salt and black pepper and mix well. Press *Power* button of "Ninja Foodi Digital Air Fry Oven" and turn the dial to select *Air Fry* mode.
- Press *Time/Slice* button and again turn the dial to set the cooking time to 15 minutes.
- Now, push *Temp/Darkness* button and rotate the dial to set the temperature at 340 Degrees °F or (171 Degrees °C).
- Press *Start/Pause* button to start your Air Fry Oven. When the unit beeps to show that it is preheated, open the oven door and grease the air fry basket.
- Arrange the kale into air fry basket and insert in the oven. When cooking time is completed, open the oven door and immediately transfer the kale mixture into a bowl.
- Stir in the cheese and lemon juice and serve hot with a garnishing of lemon zest.

Nutrition Values Per Serving: Calories: 327; Fat: 24.7g; Sat Fat: 9.5g; Carbs: 17.9g; Fiber: 2.3g; Sugar: 2.g; Protein: 11.6g

Parmesan Broccoli

Ingredients for Serving: 8

2 lbs. broccoli, cut into 1-inch florets.

¼ cup Parmesan cheese, grated.

2 tbsp. butter

Salt and ground black pepper, to taste.

Directions and Ready in About: 25-Minutes.

- In a pan of boiling water, add the broccoli and cook for about 3-4 minutes. Drain the broccoli well.
- Take a bowl, place the broccoli, cauliflower, oil, salt and black pepper and toss to coat well.
- Press *Power* button of "Ninja Foodi Digital Air Fry Oven" and turn the dial to select *Air Fry* mode. Press *Time/Slice* button and again turn the dial to set the cooking time to 15 minutes.
- Now, push *Temp/Darkness* button and rotate the dial to set the temperature at 400 Degrees °F or (204 Degrees °C).
- Press *Start/Pause* button to start your Air Fry Oven. When the unit beeps to show that it is preheated, open the oven door.
- Arrange the broccoli mixture in air fry basket and insert in the oven. Toss the broccoli mixture once halfway through.
- When cooking time is completed, open the oven door and transfer the veggie mixture into a large bowl. Immediately stir in the cheese and serve immediately with a drizzling of lemon juice.

Nutrition Values Per Serving: Calories: 73; Fat: 3.9g; Sat Fat: 2.1g; Carbs: 7.5g; Fiber: 3g; Sugar: 1.9g; Protein: 4.2g

Veggies Stuffed Bell Peppers

Ingredients for Serving: 6

1 potato, peeled and finely chopped.

1 carrot, peeled and finely chopped

1 onion, chopped finely.

6 large bell peppers.

1 bread roll, chopped finely.

½ cup fresh peas, shelled

2 garlic cloves, minced.

2 tsp. fresh parsley, chopped.

Salt and ground black pepper, to taste.

⅓ cup cheddar cheese, grated.

Directions and Ready in About: 45-Minutes.

- Remove the tops of each bell pepper and discard the seeds. Chop the bell pepper tops finely.
- Take a bowl, place bell pepper tops, bread loaf, vegetables, garlic, parsley, salt and black pepper and mix well.
- Stuff each bell pepper with the vegetable mixture. Press *Power* button of "Ninja Foodi Digital Air Fry Oven" and turn the dial to select *Air Fry* mode.
- Press *Time/Slice* button and again turn the dial to set the cooking time to 25 minutes.
- Now, push *Temp/Darkness* button and rotate the dial to set the temperature at 330 Degrees °F or (166 Degrees °C).
- Press *Start/Pause* button to start your Air Fry Oven. When the unit beeps to show that it is preheated, open the oven door.
- Arrange the bell peppers into the greased air fry basket and insert in the oven. After 20 minutes, sprinkle each bell pepper with cheddar cheese.
- When cooking time is completed, open the oven door and transfer the bell peppers onto serving plates. Serve hot with fresh salad.

Nutrition Values Per Serving: Calories: 123; Fat: 2.7g; Sat Fat: 1.2g; Carbs: 21.7g; Fiber: 3.7g; Sugar: 8g; Protein: 4.8g

Cauliflower in Buffalo Sauce

Ingredients for Serving: 4

1 large head cauliflower, cut into bite-size florets.

1 tbsp. olive oil

2 tsp. garlic powder.

Salt and ground black pepper, to taste.

⅔ cup warm buffalo sauce

Directions and Ready in About: 22-Minutes.

- Take a large bowl, add cauliflower florets, olive oil, garlic powder, salt and pepper and toss to coat. Press *Power* button of "Ninja Foodi Digital Air Fry Oven" and turn the dial to select *Air Fry* mode.
- Press *Time/Slice* button and again turn the dial to set the cooking time to 12 minutes.
- Now, push *Temp/Darkness* button and rotate the dial to set the temperature at 375 Degrees °F or (190 Degrees °C).

- Press *Start/Pause* button to start your Air Fry Oven. When the unit beeps to show that it is preheated, open the oven door.
- Arrange the cauliflower florets in the air fry basket and insert in the oven. After 7 minutes of cooking, coat the cauliflower florets with buffalo sauce.
- When cooking time is completed, open the oven door and serve hot with the garnishing of scallions.

Nutrition Values Per Serving: Calories: 183; Fat: 17.1g; Sat Fat: 4.3g; Carbs: 5.9g; Fiber: 1.8g; Sugar: 1.0g; Protein: 1.6g

Stuffed Zucchini

Ingredients for Serving: 4

4 oz. fresh mushrooms, chopped.

4 oz. goat cheese, crumbled

2 zucchinis, cut in half lengthwise.

4 oz. carrots, peeled and shredded

3 oz. onion, chopped.

12 fresh basil leaves

½ tsp. onion powder.

½ tsp. garlic powder

1 tsp. olive oil

Salt, to taste.

Directions and Ready in About: 55-Minutes.

- Carefully, scoop the flesh from the middle of each zucchini half. Season each zucchini half with a little garlic powder and salt.
- Arrange the zucchini halves into the greased sheet pan. Place the oat mixture over salmon fillets and gently, press down.
- Press *Power* button of "Ninja Foodi Digital Air Fry Oven" and turn the dial to select the *Bake* mode.
- Press *Time/Slice* button and again turn the dial to set the cooking time to 20 minutes. Now, push *Temp/Darkness* button and rotate the dial to set the temperature at 450 Degrees °F or (232 Degrees °C).
- Press *Start/Pause* button to start your Air Fry Oven. When the unit beeps to show that it is preheated, open the oven door.
- Insert the sheet pan in oven. Meanwhile, in a skillet, heat the oil over medium heat and cook the mushrooms, carrots, onions, onion powder and salt and cook for about 5-6 minutes.
- Remove from the heat and set aside. Remove the sheet pan from oven and set aside. Stuff each zucchini half with veggie mixture and top with basil leaves, followed by the cheese.
- Press *Power* button of "Ninja Foodi Digital Air Fry Oven" and turn the dial to select the *Bake* mode. Press *Time/Slice* button and again turn the dial to set the cooking time to 15 minutes.
- Now, push *Temp/Darkness* button and rotate the dial to set the temperature at 450 Degrees °F or (232 Degrees °C). Press *Start/Pause* button to start your Air Fry Oven. When the unit beeps to show that it is preheated, open the oven door.
- Insert the sheet pan in oven. When cooking time is completed, open the oven door and transfer the zucchini halves onto a platter. Serve warm alongside with fresh greens.

Nutrition Values Per Serving: Calories: 181; Fat: 11.6g; Sat Fat: 7.2g; Carbs: 10.1g; Fiber: 2.6g; Sugar: 5.3g; Protein: 11.3g

Stuffed Eggplants

Ingredients for Serving: 4

4 small eggplants, halved lengthwise.

¼ of green bell pepper, seeded and chopped

1 small onion, chopped.

½ of small tomato, chopped.

1 tbsp. fresh cilantro, chopped.

1 tbsp. cottage cheese, chopped.

1 tbsp. tomato paste

1 tsp. fresh lime juice.

1 tsp. vegetable oil

¼ tsp. garlic, chopped.

Salt and ground black pepper, to taste.

Directions and Ready in About: 31-Minutes.

- Carefully cut a slice from one side of each eggplant lengthwise. With a small spoon, scoop out the flesh from each eggplant, leaving a thick shell.
- Transfer the eggplant flesh into a bowl. Drizzle the eggplants with lime juice evenly.
- Press *Power* button of "Ninja Foodi Digital Air Fry Oven" and turn the dial to select *Air Fry* mode.
- Press *Time/Slice* button and again turn the dial to set the cooking time to 3 minutes. Now, push *Temp/Darkness* button and rotate the dial to set the temperature at 320 Degrees °F or (160 Degrees °C).
- Press *Start/Pause* button to start your Air Fry Oven. When the unit beeps to show that it is preheated, open the oven door.
- Arrange the hollowed eggplants into the greased air fry basket and insert in the oven. Meanwhile, in a skillet, heat the oil over medium heat and sauté the onion and garlic for about 2 minutes.
- Add the eggplant flesh, tomato, salt and black pepper and sauté for about 2 minutes. Stir in the cheese, bell pepper, tomato paste and cilantro and cook for about 1 minute.
- Remove the pan of the veggie mixture from heat. Once the cooking time is completed, open the oven door and arrange the cooked eggplants onto a plate.
- Stuff each eggplant with the veggie mixture. Close each with its cut part. Again arrange the eggplants shells into the greased air fry basket and insert into the oven.
- Press *Power* button of "Ninja Foodi Digital Air Fry Oven" and turn the dial to select *Air Fry* mode.
- Press *Time/Slice* button and again turn the dial to set the cooking time to 8 minutes.
- Now, push *Temp/Darkness* button and rotate the dial to set the temperature at 320 Degrees °F or (160 Degrees °C). Press *Start/Pause* button to start your Air Fry Oven.
- When cooking time is completed, open the oven door and transfer the eggplants onto serving plates. Serve hot with the topping f feta cheese.

Nutrition Values Per Serving: Calories: 131; Fat: 2g; Sat Fat: 0.3g; Carbs: 27.8g; Fiber: 5.3g; Sugar: 4.3g; Protein: 5.1g

Snacks and Appetizer Recipes

Crispy Avocado Fries

Ingredients for Serving: 2

1 avocado, peeled, pitted and sliced into 8 pieces.

½ cup panko breadcrumbs

¼ cup all-purpose flour.

1 egg

1 tsp. water

Non-stick cooking spray

Salt and ground black pepper, to taste.

Directions and Ready in About: 22-Minutes.

- Take a shallow bowl, mix the flour, salt and black pepper together. In a second bowl, mix well egg and water. In a third bowl, put the breadcrumbs.
- Coat the avocado slices with flour mixture, then dip into egg mixture and finally, coat evenly with the breadcrumbs.
- Now, spray the avocado slices evenly with cooking spray. Press *Power* button of "Ninja Foodi Digital Air Fry Oven" and turn the dial to select *Air Fry* mode.
- Press *Time/Slice* button and again turn the dial to set the cooking time to 7 minutes. Now, push *Temp/Darkness* button and rotate the dial to set the temperature at 400 Degrees °F or (204 Degrees °C).
- Press *Start/Pause* button to start your Air Fry Oven. When the unit beeps to show that it is preheated, open the oven door. Arrange the avocado fries into the air fry basket and insert in the oven.
- When cooking time is completed, open the oven door and transfer the avocado fries onto a platter. Serve warm with ketchup.

Nutrition Values Per Serving: Calories: 391; Fat: 23.8g; Sat Fat: 5.6g; Carbs: 24.8g; Fiber: 7.3g; Sugar: 0.8g; Protein: 7g

Beet Chips

Ingredients for Serving: 6

4 medium beetroots, peeled and thinly sliced.

2 tbsp. olive oil

¼ tsp. smoked paprika.

Salt, to taste.

Directions and Ready in About: 25-Minutes.

- Take a large bowl and mix all the ingredients together. Press *Power* button of "Ninja Foodi Digital Air Fry Oven" and turn the dial to select *Air Fry* mode.
- Press *Time/Slice* button and again turn the dial to set the cooking time to 15 minutes. Now, push *Temp/Darkness* button and rotate the dial to set the temperature at 325 Degrees °F or (163 Degrees °C).
- Press *Start/Pause* button to start your Air Fry Oven. When the unit beeps to show that it is preheated, open the oven door.
- Arrange the beet chips into the air fry basket and insert in the oven. Toss the beet chips once halfway through.
- When cooking time is completed, open the oven door and transfer the beet chips onto a platter. Serve at room temperature with a sprinkling of cinnamon.

Nutrition Values Per Serving: Calories: 70; Fat: 4.8g; Sat Fat: 0.7g; Carbs: 6.7g; Fiber: 1.4g; Sugar: 5.3g; Protein: 1.1g

Cheesy Broccoli Bites

Ingredients for Serving: 5

¾ cup panko breadcrumbs.

1 cup broccoli florets

¾ cup cheddar cheese, grated.

1 egg, beaten

2 tbsp. Parmesan cheese, grated.

Salt and freshly ground black pepper, as needed

Directions and Ready in About: 27-Minutes.

- In a food processor, add the broccoli and pulse until finely crumbled. Take a large bowl, mix together the broccoli and remaining ingredients.
- Make small equal-sized balls from the mixture. Press *Power* button of "Ninja Foodi Digital Air Fry Oven" and turn the dial to select *Air Fry* mode.
- Press *Time/Slice* button and again turn the dial to set the cooking time to 12 minutes. Now, push *Temp/Darkness* button and rotate the dial to set the temperature at 350 Degrees °F or (176 Degrees °C).
- Press *Start/Pause* button to start your Air Fry Oven. When the unit beeps to show that it is preheated, open the oven door.
- Arrange the broccoli balls into the air fry basket and insert in the oven. When cooking time is completed, open the oven door and transfer the broccoli bites onto a platter. Serve warm with your favorite dipping sauce.

Nutrition Values Per Serving: Calories: 153; Fat: .2g; Sat Fat: 4.5g; Carbs: 4g; Fiber: 0.5g; Sugar: 0.5g; Protein: 7.1g

Risotto Bites

Ingredients for Serving: 4

1½ oz. mozzarella cheese, cubed.

1½ cups cooked risotto

½ egg, beaten.

⅓ cup breadcrumbs

3 tbsp. Parmesan cheese, grated.

Directions and Ready in About: 25-Minutes.

- Take a bowl, add the risotto, Parmesan and egg and mix until well combined. Make 20 equal-sized balls from the mixture.
- Insert a mozzarella cube in the center of each ball. With your fingers smooth the risotto mixture to cover the ball.
- In a shallow dish, place the breadcrumbs. Coat the balls with the breadcrumbs evenly. Press *Power* button of "Ninja Foodi Digital Air Fry Oven" and turn the dial to select *Air Fry* mode.
- Press *Time/Slice* button and again turn the dial to set the cooking time to 10 minutes. Now, push *Temp/Darkness* button and rotate the dial to set the temperature at 390 Degrees °F or (199 Degrees °C).
- Press *Start/Pause* button to start your Air Fry Oven. When the unit beeps to show that it is preheated, open the oven door. Arrange the balls into the air fry basket and insert in the oven.

- When cooking time is completed, open the oven door and transfer the risotto bites onto a platter. Serve warm with blue cheese dip.

Nutrition Values Per Serving: Calories: 340; Fat: 4.3g; Sat Fat: 2g; Carbs: 62.4g; Fiber: 1.3g; Sugar: 0.7g; Protein: 11.3g

Potato Croquettes

Ingredients for Serving: 4

2 medium Russet potatoes, peeled and cubed

½ cup breadcrumbs.

½ cup Parmesan cheese, grated.

2 eggs

1 egg yolk

2 tbsp. vegetable oil

2 tbsp. fresh chives, minced.

2 tbsp. all-purpose flour.

Pinch of ground nutmeg

Salt and freshly ground black pepper, as needed.

Directions and Ready in About: 23-Minutes.

- In a pan of a boiling water, add the potatoes and cook for about 15 minutes. Drain the potatoes well and transfer into a large bowl.
- With a potato masher, mash the potatoes and set aside to cool completely.
- In the bowl of mashed potatoes, add the flour, Parmesan cheese, egg yolk, chives, nutmeg, salt and black pepper and mix until well combined. Make small equal-sized balls from the mixture.
- Now, roll each ball into a cylinder shape. In a shallow dish, crack the eggs and beat well. In another dish, mix together the breadcrumbs and oil.
- Dip the croquettes in egg mixture and then coat with the breadcrumbs mixture. Press *Power* button of "Ninja Foodi Digital Air Fry Oven" and turn the dial to select *Air Fry* mode.
- Press *Time/Slice* button and again turn the dial to set the cooking time to 8 minutes.
- Now, push *Temp/Darkness* button and rotate the dial to set the temperature at 390 Degrees °F or (199 Degrees °C). Press *Start/Pause* button to start your Air Fry Oven.
- When the unit beeps to show that it is preheated, open the oven door. Arrange the croquettes in air fry basket and insert in the oven.
- When cooking time is completed, open the oven door and transfer the croquettes onto a platter. Serve warm with mustard sauce.

Nutrition Values Per Serving: Calories: 283; Fat: 13.4g; Sat Fat: 3.8g; Carbs: 29.9g; Fiber: 3.3g; Sugar: 2.3g; Protein: 11.5g

Cod Nuggets

Ingredients for Serving: 5

1 lb. cod, cut into 1x2½-inch strips.

¾ cup breadcrumbs

2 eggs

1 cup all-purpose flour.

2 tbsp. olive oil

Pinch of salt

Directions and Ready in About: 23-Minutes.

- In a shallow dish, place the flour. Crack the eggs in a second dish and beat well. In a third dish, mix together the breadcrumbs, salt and oil.
- Coat the nuggets with flour, then dip into beaten eggs and finally, coat with the breadcrumbs. Press *Power* button of "Ninja Foodi Digital Air Fry Oven" and turn the dial to select *Air Fry* mode.
- Press *Time/Slice* button and again turn the dial to set the cooking time to 8 minutes. Now, push *Temp/Darkness* button and rotate the dial to set the temperature at 390 Degrees °F or (199 Degrees °C).
- Press *Start/Pause* button to start your Air Fry Oven. When the unit beeps to show that it is preheated, open the oven door.
- Arrange the nuggets in air fry basket and insert in the oven. When cooking time is completed, open the oven door and transfer the nuggets onto a platter. Serve warm with tartar sauce.

Nutrition Values Per Serving: Calories: 323; Fat: 9.2g; Sat Fat: 1.7g; Carbs: 30.9g; Fiber: 1.4g; Sugar: 1.2g; Protein: 27.7g

Beef Taquitos

Ingredients for Serving: 6

2 cups cooked beef, shredded.

1 cup pepper jack cheese, shredded.

½ cup onion, chopped.

6 corn tortillas

Olive oil cooking spray

Directions and Ready in About: 23-Minutes.

- Arrange the tortillas onto a smooth surface. Place the shredded meat over one corner of each tortilla, followed by onion and cheese.
- Roll each tortilla to secure the filling and secure with toothpicks. Spray each taquito with cooking spray evenly.
- Arrange the taquitos onto the greased sheet pan. Place the tofu mixture in the greased sheet pan. Press *Power* button of "Ninja Foodi Digital Air Fry Oven" and turn the dial to select *Air Fry* mode.
- Press *Time/Slice* button and again turn the dial to set the cooking time to 8 minutes. Now, push *Temp/Darkness* button and rotate the dial to set the temperature at 400 Degrees °F or (204 Degrees °C).
- Press *Start/Pause* button to start your Air Fry Oven. When the unit beeps to show that it is preheated, open the oven door and insert the sheet pan in oven.
- When cooking time is completed, open the oven door and transfer the taquitos onto a platter. Serve warm with yogurt dip.

Nutrition Values Per Serving: Calories: 228| Fat: 9.6g; Sat Fat: 4.8g; Carbs: 12.3g; Fiber: 1.7g; Sugar: 0.6g; Protein: 22.7g

Tortilla Chips

Ingredients for Serving: 3

4 corn tortillas, cut into triangles.

1 tbsp. olive oil

Salt, to taste.

Directions and Ready in About: 13-Minutes.

- Coat the tortilla chips with oil and then sprinkle each side of the tortillas with salt. Press *Power* button of "Ninja Foodi Digital Air Fry Oven" and turn the dial to select *Air Fry* mode.
- Press *Time/Slice* button and again turn the dial to set the cooking time to 3 minutes. Now, push *Temp/Darkness* button and rotate the dial to set the temperature at 390 Degrees °F or (199 Degrees °C).
- Press *Start/Pause* button to start your Air Fry Oven. When the unit beeps to show that it is preheated, open the oven door.
- Arrange the tortilla chips in air fry basket and insert in the oven. When cooking time is completed, open the oven door and transfer the tortilla chips onto a platter. Serve warm with guacamole.

Nutrition Values Per Serving: Calories: 110; Fat: 5.6g; Sat Fat: 0.8g; Carbs: 14.3g; Fiber: 2g; Sugar: 0.3g; Protein: 1.8g

Spicy Carrot Fries

Ingredients for Serving: 2

1 large carrot, peeled and cut into sticks.

1 tbsp. fresh rosemary, chopped finely.

1 tbsp. olive oil

¼ tsp. cayenne pepper

Salt and ground black pepper, to taste.

Directions and Ready in About: 22-Minutes.

- Take a bowl, add all the ingredients and mix well. Press *Power* button of "Ninja Foodi Digital Air Fry Oven" and turn the dial to select *Air Fry* mode.
- Press *Time/Slice* button and again turn the dial to set the cooking time to 12 minutes. Now, push *Temp/Darkness* button and rotate the dial to set the temperature at 390 Degrees °F or (199 Degrees °C).
- Press *Start/Pause* button to start your Air Fry Oven. When the unit beeps to show that it is preheated, open the oven door.
- Arrange the carrot fries into the air fry basket and insert in the oven. When cooking time is completed, open the oven door and transfer the carrot fries onto a platter. Serve warm with mustard sauce.

Nutrition Values Per Serving: Calories: 81; Fat: 8.3g; Sat Fat: 1.1g; Carbs: 4.7g; Fiber: 1.7g; Sugar: 1.8g; Protein: 0.4g

Avocado Fries

Ingredients for Serving: 4

½ cup panko breadcrumbs.

1 cup egg, whisked

½ tsp. salt

1 avocado, peeled, pitted and sliced.

Directions and Ready in About: 35-Minutes.

- Toss breadcrumbs with salt in a shallow bowl. First, dip the avocado strips in the egg, then coat them with panko. Spread these slices in the air fry basket.
- Transfer the sandwich to the "Ninja Foodi Digital Air Fry Oven" and close the door. Select *Bake* mode by rotating the dial.
- Press the *Time/Slice* button and change the value to 20 minutes. Press the *Temp/Darkness* button and change the value to 400 Degrees °F or (204 Degrees °C).
- Press *Start/Pause* to begin cooking. Serve fresh with chili sauce or mayonnaise dip.

Nutrition Values Per Serving: Calories: 110; Fat: 9g; Sodium: 318mg; Carbs: 19g; Fiber: 5g; Sugar: 3g; Protein: 7g

Ranch Kale Chips

Ingredients for Serving: 6

4 cups kale leaves.

2 tbsp. olive oil

1 tbsp. nutritional yeast flakes.

2 tsp. Vegan Ranch Seasoning

¼ tsp. salt

Directions and Ready in About: 20-Minutes.

- Toss the kale leaves with oil, salt, yeast and Ranch seasoning in a large bowl. Spread the seasoned kale leaves in the air fry basket.
- Transfer the air fry basket to the "Ninja Foodi Digital Air Fry Oven" and close the door. Select *Air Fry* mode by rotating the dial. Press the *Time/Slice* button and change the value to 5 minutes.
- Press the *Temp/Darkness* button and change the value to 370 Degrees °F or (187 Degrees °C). Press *Start/Pause* to begin cooking. Serve warm with a cream cheese dip on the side.

Nutrition Values Per Serving: Calories: 123; Fat: 8g; Sodium: 146mg; Carbs: 8g; Fiber: 5g; Sugar: 1g; Protein: 7g

Onion Rings

Ingredients for Serving: 4

½ cup buttermilk.

½ cup all-purpose flour

1 large yellow sweet onion, sliced. ½-inch-thick rings.

1 cup panko breadcrumbs.

1 egg

2 tbsp. olive oil

1 tsp. paprika

1 tsp. salt, divided.

Directions and Ready in About: 30-Minutes.

- Mix flour with paprika and salt on a plate. Coat the onion rings with the flour mixture. Beat egg with buttermilk in a bowl. Dip all the onion rings with the egg mixture.
- Spread the breadcrumbs in a bowl. Coat the onion rings with breadcrumbs. Place the onion rings in the air fry basket and spray them with cooking oil.
- Transfer the basket to the "Ninja Foodi Digital Air Fry Oven" and close the door. Select *Air Fry* mode by rotating the dial. Press the *Temp/Darkness* button and change the value to 400 Degrees °F or (204 Degrees °C).

- Press the *Time/Slice* button and change the value to 15 minutes, then press *Start/Pause* to begin cooking. Serve warm with chili sauce or mayo dip.

Nutrition Values Per Serving: Calories: 106; Fat: 5g; Sodium: 244mg; Carbs: 16g; Fiber: 1g; Sugar: 1g; Protein: 7g

Baked Potatoes

Ingredients for Serving: 3

3 russet potatoes, scrubbed and rinsed.

½ tsp. garlic powder

½ tsp. sea salt.

Cooking spray

Directions and Ready in About: 1 hr.

- Rub the potatoes with salt and garlic powder. Place the potatoes in the air fry basket and spray with cooking spray. Transfer the basket to the "Ninja Foodi Digital Air Fry Oven" and close the door.
- Select the *Bake* mode by rotating the dial. Press the *Time/Slice* button and change the value to 45 minutes.
- Press the *Temp/Darkness* button and change the value to 350 Degrees °F or (176 Degrees °C). Press *Start/Pause* to begin cooking. Make a slit on top of potatoes and score the flesh inside. Serve warm with butter sauce or mayo dip.

Nutrition Values Per Serving: Calories: 269; Fat: 5g; Sodium: 510mg; Carbs: 37g; Fiber: 5g; Sugar: 4g; Protein: 1g

Potato Bread Rolls

Ingredients for Serving: 8

5 large potatoes, peeled.

8 bread slices, trimmed

2 small onions, chopped finely.

2 green chilies, seeded and chopped.

2 curry leaves

2 tbsp. vegetable oil, divided.

½ tsp. ground turmeric

Salt, to taste.

Directions and Ready in About: 53-Minutes.

- In a pan of boiling water, add the potatoes and cook for about 15-20 minutes. Drain the potatoes well and with a potato masher, mash the potatoes.
- In a skillet, heat 1 tsp. of oil over medium heat and sauté the onion for about 4-5 minutes. Add the green chilies, curry leaves and turmeric and sauté for about 1 minute.
- Add the mashed potatoes and salt and mix well. Remove from the heat and set aside to cool completely. Make 8 equal-sized oval-shaped patties from the mixture.
- Wet the bread slices completely with water. Press each bread slice between your hands to remove the excess water. Place 1 bread slice in your palm and place 1 patty in the center of the bread.
- Roll the bread slice in a spindle shape and seal the edges to secure the filling. Coat the roll with some oil.
- Repeat with the remaining slices, filling and oil. Press *Power* button of "Ninja Foodi Digital Air Fry Oven" and turn the dial to select *Air Fry* mode.
- Press *Time/Slice* button and again turn the dial to set the cooking time to 13 minutes. Now, push

Temp/Darkness button and rotate the dial to set the temperature at 390 Degrees °F or (199 Degrees °C).
- Press *Start/Pause* button to start your Air Fry Oven. When the unit beeps to show that it is preheated, open the oven door.
- Arrange the bread rolls into the air fry basket and insert in the oven. When cooking time is completed, open the oven door and transfer the rolls onto a platter. Serve warm with alongside the ketchup.

Nutrition Values Per Serving: Calories: 222; Fat: 4g; Sat Fat: 0.8g; Carbs: 42.5g; Fiber: 6.2g; Sugar: 3.8g; Protein: 4.8g

Zucchini Fries

Ingredients for Serving: 4

1 lb. zucchini, sliced. into 2½-inch sticks.

2 tbsp. olive oil.

¾ cup panko breadcrumbs

Salt, to taste.

Directions and Ready in About: 22-Minutes.

- In a colander, add the zucchini and sprinkle with salt. Set aside for about 10 minutes. Gently pat dry the zucchini sticks with the paper towels and coat with oil.
- In a shallow dish, add the breadcrumbs. Coat the zucchini sticks with breadcrumbs evenly. Press *Power* button of "Ninja Foodi Digital Air Fry Oven" and turn the dial to select *Air Fry* mode.
- Press *Time/Slice* button and again turn the dial to set the cooking time to 12 minutes. Now, push *Temp/Darkness* button and rotate the dial to set the temperature at 400 Degrees °F or (204 Degrees °C).
- Press *Start/Pause* button to start your Air Fry Oven. When the unit beeps to show that it is preheated, open the oven door.
- Arrange the zucchini fries in air fry basket and insert in the oven. When cooking time is completed, open the oven door and transfer the zucchini fries onto a platter. Serve warm with ketchup.

Nutrition Values Per Serving: Calories: 151; Fat: 8.6g; Sat Fat: 1.6g; Carbs: 6.9g; Fiber: 1.3g; Sugar: 2g; Protein: 1.9g

Spicy Spinach Chips

Ingredients for Serving: 4

2 cups fresh spinach leaves, torn into bite-sized pieces.

½ tbsp. coconut oil, melted

⅛ tsp. garlic powder.

Salt, to taste.

Directions and Ready in About: 10-Minutes.

- Take a large bowl and mix together all the ingredients. Arrange the spinach pieces onto the greased sheet pan. Press *Power* button of "Ninja Foodi Digital Air Fry Oven" and turn the dial to select *Air Fry* mode.
- Press *Time/Slice* button and again turn the dial to set the cooking time to 10 minutes. Now, push *Temp/Darkness* button and rotate the dial to set the temperature at 300 Degrees °F or (149 Degrees °C).

- Press *Start/Pause* button to start your Air Fry Oven. When the unit beeps to show that it is preheated, open the oven door.
- Insert the sheet pan in oven. Toss the spinach chips once halfway through. When cooking time is completed, open the oven door and transfer the spinach chips onto a platter. Serve warm with a sprinkling of cayenne pepper.

Nutrition Values Per Serving: Calories: 18; Fat: 1.5g; Sat Fat: 0g; Carbs: 0.5g; Fiber: 0.3g; Sugar: 0.1g; Protein: 0.5g

Pumpkin Fries

Ingredients for Serving: 6

½ cup plain Greek yogurt.

1 medium pie pumpkin

2 tbsp. maple syrup.

3 tsp. chipotle peppers in adobo sauce, minced.

¼ tsp. ground cumin.

¼ tsp. chili powder

¼ tsp. pepper.

¼ tsp. garlic powder

⅛ tsp. salt

Directions and Ready in About: 27-Minutes.

- Peel and cut the pumpkin into sticks. Mix garlic powder, cumin, chili powder, salt and black pepper. Coat the pumpkin sticks with the spice mixture.
- Spread the pumpkin fries in the air fry basket and spray them with cooking spray. Transfer the basket to the "Ninja Foodi Digital Air Fry Oven" and close the door.
- Select *Air Fry* mode by rotating the dial. Press the *Time/Slice* button and change the value to 12 minutes.
- Press the *Temp/Darkness* button and change the value to 400 Degrees °F or (204 Degrees °C). Press *Start/Pause* to begin cooking.
- Toss the fries once cooked halfway through, then resume cooking. Mix yogurt with maple syrup and adobo sauce in a bowl. Serve fries with the sauce or with tomato ketchup.

Nutrition Values Per Serving: Calories: 215; Fat: 16g; Sodium: 255mg; Carbs: 31g; Fiber: 1.2g; Sugar: 5g; Protein: 4.1g

Crispy Prawns

Ingredients for Serving: 4

12 prawns, peeled and deveined

1 egg

½ lb. nacho chips, crushed.

Directions and Ready in About: 23-Minutes.

- In a shallow dish, beat the egg. In another shallow dish, place the crushed nacho chips. Coat the prawn with the beaten egg and then roll into nacho chips.
- Press *Power* button of "Ninja Foodi Digital Air Fry Oven" and turn the dial to select *Air Fry* mode. Press *Time/Slice* button and again turn the dial to set the cooking time to 8 minutes.
- Now, push *Temp/Darkness* button and rotate the dial to set the temperature at 355 Degrees °F or (179 Degrees °C). Press *Start/Pause* button to start your Air Fry Oven.
- When the unit beeps to show that it is preheated, open the oven door. Arrange the prawns into the air fry basket and insert in the oven.

- When cooking time is completed, open the oven door and serve immediately with alongside your favorite dip.

Nutrition Values Per Serving: Calories: 386; Fat: 17g; Sat Fat: 2.9g; Carbs: 36.1g; Fiber: 2.6g; Sugar: 2.2g; Protein: 21g

Cheesy Chicken Nuggets

Ingredients for Serving: 6

2 large chicken breasts, cut into 1-inch cubes.

1 cup breadcrumbs

⅓ tbsp. Parmesan cheese, shredded.

¼ tsp. smoked paprika

1 tsp. onion powder.

Salt and ground black pepper, to taste.

Directions and Ready in About: 25-Minutes.

- In a large resealable bag, add all the ingredients. Seal the bag and shake well to coat completely. Press *Power* button of "Ninja Foodi Digital Air Fry Oven" and turn the dial to select *Air Fry* mode.
- Press *Time/Slice* button and again turn the dial to set the cooking time to 10 minutes. Now, push *Temp/Darkness* button and rotate the dial to set the temperature at 400 Degrees °F or (204 Degrees °C).
- Press *Start/Pause* button to start your Air Fry Oven. When the unit beeps to show that it is preheated, open the oven door.
- Arrange the nuggets into the air fry basket and insert in the oven. When cooking time is completed, open the oven door and transfer the nuggets onto a platter. Serve warm with mustard sauce.

Nutrition Values Per Serving: Calories: 218; Fat: 6.6g; Sat Fat: 1.8g; Carbs: 13.3g; Fiber: 0.9g; Sugar: 1.3g; Protein: 24.4g

Persimmon Chips

Ingredients for Serving: 2

2 ripe persimmons, cut into slices horizontally

Salt and ground black pepper, to taste.

Directions and Ready in About: 20-Minutes.

- Arrange the persimmons slices onto the greased sheet pan. Press *Power* button of "Ninja Foodi Digital Air Fry Oven" and turn the dial to select *Air Fry* mode.
- Press *Time/Slice* button and again turn the dial to set the cooking time to 10 minutes. Now, push *Temp/Darkness* button and rotate the dial to set the temperature at 400 Degrees °F or (204 Degrees °C).
- Press *Start/Pause* button to start your Air Fry Oven. When the unit beeps to show that it is preheated, open the oven door.
- Insert the sheet pan in oven. Flip the chips once halfway through. When cooking time is completed, open the oven door and transfer the chips onto a platter. Serve warm with a sprinkling of ground cinnamon.

Nutrition Values Per Serving: Calories: 32; Fat: 0.1g; Sat Fat: 0g; Carbs: 8.4g; Fiber: 0g; Sugar: 0g; Protein: 0.2g

Carrot Chips

Ingredients for Serving: 8

2 lbs. carrots, sliced.

¼ cup olive oil

1 tbsp. sea salt.

1 tsp. ground cinnamon

1 tsp. ground cumin.

Directions and Ready in About: 30-Minutes.

- Toss the carrot slices with oil, sea salt, cumin and cinnamon in a large bowl. Grease the sheet pan and spread the carrot slices in it.
- Transfer the sheet pan to the "Ninja Foodi Digital Air Fry Oven" and close the door. Select *Bake* mode by rotating the dial.
- Press the *Time/Slice* button and change the value to 15 minutes. Press the *Temp/Darkness* button and change the value to 450 Degrees °F or (232 Degrees °C).
- Press *Start/Pause* to begin cooking. Flip the chips after 7-8 minutes of cooking and resume baking. Serve fresh with tomato ketchup or cheese dip.

Nutrition Values Per Serving: Calories: 182; Fat: 2g; Sodium: 350mg; Carbs: 12.2g; Fiber: 0.7g; Sugar: 1g; Protein: 4.3g

Air Roasted Cashews

Ingredients for Serving: 6

1½ cups raw cashew nuts.

1 tsp. butter, melted

Salt and freshly ground black pepper, to taste.

Directions and Ready in About: 10-Minutes.

- Take a bowl, mix all the ingredients together. Press *Power* button of "Ninja Foodi Digital Air Fry Oven" and turn the dial to select *Air Fry* mode.
- Press *Time/Slice* button and again turn the dial to set the cooking time to 5 minutes. Now, push *Temp/Darkness* button and rotate the dial to set the temperature at 355 Degrees °F or (179 Degrees °C).
- Press *Start/Pause* button to start your Air Fry Oven. When the unit beeps to show that it is preheated, open the oven door.
- Arrange the cashews into the air fry basket and insert in the oven. Shake the cashews once halfway through.
- When cooking time is completed, open the oven door and transfer the cashews into a heatproof bowl. Serve warm with a sprinkling of little salt.

Nutrition Values Per Serving: Calories: 202; Fat: 16.5g; Sat Fat: 3.5g; Carbs: 11.2g; Fiber: 1g; Sugar: 1.7g; Protein: 5.3g

Pasta Chips

Ingredients for Serving: 4

1 cup bow tie pasta.

½ tbsp. olive oil

½ tbsp. nutritional yeast.

⅔ tsp. Italian Seasoning Blend

¼ tsp. salt

Directions and Ready in About: 25-Minutes.

- Cook and boil the pasta in salted water in half of the time as stated on the box, then drain it. Toss the boiled pasta

with salt, Italian seasoning, nutritional yeast and olive oil in a bowl.
- Spread this pasta in the air fry basket. Transfer the basket to the "Ninja Foodi Digital Air Fry Oven" and close the door.
- Select *Air Fry* mode by rotating the dial. Press the *Time/Slice* button and change the value to 5 minutes.
- Press the *Temp/Darkness* button and change the value to 390 Degrees °F or (199 Degrees °C).
- Press *Start/Pause* to begin cooking. Toss the pasta and continue air frying for another 5 minutes. Serve the chips with white cheese dip.

Nutrition Values Per Serving: Calories: 167; Fat: 2g; Sodium: 48mg; Carbs: 26g; Fiber: 2g; Sugar: 0g; Protein: 1g

Glazed Chicken Wings

Ingredients for Serving: 4

1½ lbs. chicken wingettes and drumettes

⅓ cup tomato sauce.

2 tbsp. maple syrup

2 tbsp. balsamic vinegar.

½ tsp. liquid smoke

¼ tsp. red pepper flakes, crushed.

Salt, to taste.

- Directions and Ready in About: 40-Minutes.
- Arrange the wings onto the greased sheet pan. Press *Power* button of "Ninja Foodi Digital Air Fry Oven" and turn the dial to select *Air Fry* mode.
- Press *Time/Slice* button and again turn the dial to set the cooking time to 25 minutes. Now, push *Temp/Darkness* button and rotate the dial to set the temperature at 380 Degrees °F or (193 Degrees °C).
- Press *Start/Pause* button to start your Air Fry Oven. When the unit beeps to show that it is preheated, open the oven door and insert the sheet pan in oven.
- Meanwhile, in a small pan, add the remaining ingredients over medium heat and cook for about 10 minutes, stirring occasionally.
- When cooking time is completed, open the oven door and place the chicken wings into a bowl. Add the sauce and toss to coat well. Serve immediately with your favorite dip.

Nutrition Values Per Serving: Calories: 356; Fat: 12.7g; Sat Fat: 3.5g; Carbs: 7.9g; Fiber: 0.3g; Sugar: 6.9g; Protein: 49.5g

Buttermilk Biscuits

Ingredients for Serving: 8

¼ cup cold unsalted butter, cut into cubes.

¾ cup buttermilk

½ cup cake flour.

1¼ cups all-purpose flour

2 tbsp. butter, melted.

¼ tsp. baking soda

½ tsp. baking powder.

1 tsp. granulated sugar

Salt, to taste.

Directions and Ready in About: 23-Minutes.

- Take a large bowl, sift together flours, baking soda, baking powder, sugar and salt. With a pastry cutter, cut cold butter and mix until coarse crumb forms.

- Slowly, add buttermilk and mix until a smooth dough forms. Place the dough onto a floured surface and with your hands, press it into ½-inch thickness.
- With a 1¾-inch-round cookie cutter, cut the biscuits. Arrange the biscuits into a sheet pan in a single layer and coat with the butter.
- Press *Power* button of "Ninja Foodi Digital Air Fry Oven" and turn the dial to select *Air Fry* mode. Press *Time/Slice* button and again turn the dial to set the cooking time to 8 minutes.
- Now, push *Temp/Darkness* button and rotate the dial to set the temperature at 400 Degrees °F or (204 Degrees °C). Press *Start/Pause* button to start your Air Fry Oven. When the unit beeps to show that it is preheated, open the oven door.
- Arrange pan over the wire rack and insert in the oven. When cooking time is completed, open the oven door and place the sheet pan onto a wire rack for about 5 minutes.
- Carefully invert the biscuits onto the wire rack to cool completely before serving. Serve with the drizzling of melted butter.

Nutrition Values Per Serving: Calories: 187; Fat: 9.1g; Sat Fat: 5.6g; Carbs: 22.6g; Fiber: 0.8g; Sugar: 1.7g; Protein: 3.7g

Eggplant Fries

Ingredients for Serving: 4

1 (1¼-pound) eggplant, peeled.	2 large eggs
½ cup grated Parmesan cheese	½ cup toasted wheat germ
	1 tsp. Italian seasoning.
1 cup meatless pasta sauce, warmed.	¾ tsp. garlic salt
	Cooking spray

Directions and Ready in About: 25-Minutes.

- Cut the eggplant into sticks. Mix parmesan cheese, wheat germ, seasoning and garlic salt in a bowl. Coat the eggplant sticks with the parmesan mixture.
- Place the eggplant fries in the air fry basket and spray them with cooking spray. Transfer the basket to the "Ninja Foodi Digital Air Fry Oven" and close the door.
- Select *Air Fry* mode by rotating the dial. Press the *Time/Slice* button and change the value to 10 minutes.
- Press the *Temp/Darkness* button and change the value to 375 Degrees °F or (190 Degrees °C). Press *Start/Pause* to begin cooking. Serve warm with marinara sauce or with tomato sauce.

Nutrition Values Per Serving: Calories: 201; Fat: 7g; Sodium: 269mg; Carbs: 35g; Fiber: 4g; Sugar: 12g; Protein: 6g

Roasted Peanuts

Ingredients for Serving: 6

1½ cups raw peanuts.	Nonstick cooking spray

Directions and Ready in About: 19-Minutes.

- Press *Power* button of "Ninja Foodi Digital Air Fry Oven" and turn the dial to select *Air Fry* mode. Press

Time/Slice button and again turn the dial to set the cooking time to 14 minutes.
- Now, push *Temp/Darkness* button and rotate the dial to set the temperature at 320 Degrees °F or (160 Degrees °C). Press *Start/Pause* button to start your Air Fry Oven. When the unit beeps to show that it is preheated, open the oven door.
- Arrange the peanuts in air fry basket and insert in the oven. While cooking, toss the peanuts twice. After 9 minutes of cooking, spray the peanuts with cooking spray.
- When cooking time is completed, open the oven door and transfer the peanuts into a heatproof bowl. Serve warm with a sprinkling of little cinnamon.

Nutrition Values Per Serving: Calories: 207; Fat: 18g; Sat Fat: 2.5g; Carbs: 5.9g; Fiber: 3.1g; Sugar: 1.5g; Protein: 9.4g

Potato Chips

Ingredients for Serving: 2

1 medium Russet potato, sliced.	¼ tsp. sea salt
	1 tsp. chopped fresh rosemary.
1 tbsp. canola oil	
¼ tsp. black pepper.	

Directions and Ready in About: 40-Minutes.

- Fill a suitable glass bowl with cold water and add sliced potatoes. Leave the potatoes for 20 minutes, then drain them. Pat dry the chips with a paper towel.
- Toss the potatoes with salt, black pepper and oil to coat well. Spread the potato slices in the air fry basket evenly. Transfer the basket to the "Ninja Foodi Digital Air Fry Oven" and close the door.
- Select *Air Fry* mode by rotating the dial. Press the *Time/Slice* button and change the value to 25 minutes.
- Press the *Temp/Darkness* button and change the value to 375 Degrees °F or (190 Degrees °C). Press *Start/Pause* to begin cooking. Garnish with rosemary. Serve warm with tomato sauce.

Nutrition Values Per Serving: Calories: 134; Fat: 3g; Sodium: 216mg; Carbs: 27g; Fiber: 3g; Sugar: 4g; Protein: 1g

Fiesta Chicken Fingers

Ingredients for Serving: 4

¾ lb. boneless chicken breasts, cut into strips.	3 cups corn chips, crushed
	½ cup buttermilk.
1 cup all-purpose flour	¼ tsp. pepper
1 envelope taco seasoning.	

For Serving:

Sour cream ranch dip or Fresh salsa

Directions and Ready in About: 27-Minutes.

- Coat the chicken with pepper and flour. Mix corn chips with taco seasoning. Dip the chicken fingers in the buttermilk, then coat with the corn chips.

- Place the chicken fingers in the air fry basket and spray with cooking oil. Transfer the basket to the "Ninja Foodi Digital Air Fry Oven" and close the door.
- Select *Air Fry* mode by rotating the dial. Press the *Time/Slice* button and change the value to 12 minutes.
- Press the *Temp/Darkness* button and change the value to 325 Degrees °F or (163 Degrees °C). Press *Start/Pause* to begin cooking. Flip the Chicken fingers once cooked halfway through, then resume cooking.
- Serve warm with sour cream ranch dip or fresh salsa or with chili garlic sauce.

Nutrition Values Per Serving: Calories: 218; Fat: 12g; Sodium: 710mg; Carbs: 44g; Fiber: 5g; Sugar: 3g; Protein: 24g

Mini Hot Dogs

Ingredients for Serving: 8

8 oz. refrigerated crescent rolls

24 cocktail hot dogs.

Directions and Ready in About: 19-Minutes.

- Spread the crescent rolls into 8 triangles and cut each into 3 triangles. Place one mini hot dog at the center of each crescent roll.
- Wrap the rolls around the hot dog and place them in the air fry basket. Transfer the basket to the "Ninja Foodi Digital Air Fry Oven" and close the door.
- Select *Air Fry* mode by rotating the dial. Press the *Time/Slice* button and change the value to 4 minutes.
- Press the *Temp/Darkness* button and change the value to 325 Degrees °F or (163 Degrees °C). Press *Start/Pause* to begin cooking. Serve warm with tomato ketchup or cream cheese dip.

Nutrition Values Per Serving: Calories: 152; Fat: 4g; Sodium: 232mg; Carbs: 17g; Fiber: 1g; Sugar: 0g; Protein: 24g

Cauliflower Poppers

Ingredients for Serving: 6

1 medium head cauliflower, cut into florets.

3 tbsp. olive oil

½ tsp. ground cumin.

¼ tsp. ground turmeric

1 tsp. paprika

Salt and ground black pepper, to taste.

Directions and Ready in About: 30-Minutes.

- Take a bowl, place all ingredients and toss to coat well. Place the cauliflower mixture in the greased sheet pan. Press *Power* button of "Ninja Foodi Digital Air Fry Oven" and turn the dial to select the *Bake* mode.
- Press *Time/Slice* button and again turn the dial to set the cooking time to 20 minutes. Now, push *Temp/Darkness* button and rotate the dial to set the temperature at 450 Degrees °F or (232 Degrees °C).
- Press *Start/Pause* button to start your Air Fry Oven. When the unit beeps to show that it is preheated, open the oven door and insert the sheet pan in oven.
- Flip the cauliflower mixture once halfway through. When cooking time is completed, open the oven door and transfer the cauliflower poppers onto a platter. Serve warm with a squeeze of lemon juice.

Nutrition Values Per Serving: Calories: 73; Fat: 7.1g; Sat Fat: 1g; Carbs: 2.7g; Fiber: 1.3g; Sugar: 1.1g; Protein: 1g

Dessert Recipes

Chocolate Chip Cookie

Ingredients for Serving: 6

½ cup butter, softened.

½ cup sugar.

1 cup chocolate chips

1 tsp. vanilla

1 ½ cups all-purpose flour.

½ tsp. baking soda.

½ cup brown sugar

¼ tsp. salt

1 egg

Directions and Ready in About: 27-Minutes.

- Grease the sheet pan with cooking spray. Beat butter with sugar and brown sugar in a mixing bowl. Stir in vanilla, egg, salt, flour and baking soda, then mix well. Fold in chocolate chips, then knead this dough a bit. Spread the prepared dough in the prepared sheet pan evenly.
- Transfer the pan to the "Ninja Foodi Digital Air Fry Oven" and close the door. Select *Bake* mode by rotating the dial. Press the *Time/Slice* button and change the value to 12 minutes. Press the *Temp/Darkness* button and change the value to 400 Degrees °F or (204 Degrees °C). Press *Start/Pause* to begin cooking. Serve oven fresh with warm milk.

Nutrition Values Per Serving: Calories: 173; Fat: 12g; Sodium: 79mg; Carbs: 24.8g; Fiber: 1.1g; Sugar: 18g; Protein: 15g

Strawberry Cupcakes

Ingredients for Serving: 10

For Cupcakes:

⅞ cup self-rising flour.

7 tbsp. butter

2 eggs

½ tsp. vanilla essence.

½ cup caster sugar.

For Frosting:

¼ cup fresh strawberries, pureed.

1 tbsp. whipped cream.

1 cup icing sugar

3½ tbsp. butter

½ tsp. pink food color.

- Directions and Ready in About: 28-Minutes.
- Take a bowl, add the butter and sugar and beat until fluffy and light. Add the eggs, one at a time and beat until well combined. Stir in the vanilla extract. Gradually, add the flour, beating continuously until well combined.
- Place the mixture into 10 silicone cups. Press *Power* button of "Ninja Foodi Digital Air Fry Oven" and turn the dial to select *Air Fry* mode. Press *Time/Slice* button and again turn the dial to set the cooking time to 8 minutes.
- Now, push *Temp/Darkness* button and rotate the dial to set the temperature at 340 Degrees °F or (171 Degrees °C). Press *Start/Pause* button to start your Air Fry Oven. When the unit beeps to show that it is preheated, open the oven door.

- Arrange the silicone cups into the air fry basket and insert in the oven. When cooking time is completed, open the oven door and place the silicon cups onto a wire rack to cool for about 10 minutes.
- Carefully invert the muffins onto the wire rack to completely cool before frosting. For frosting: in a bowl, add the icing sugar and butter and whisk until fluffy and light.
- Add the whipped cream, strawberry puree and color. Mix until well combined. Fill the pastry bag with frosting and decorate the cupcakes. Serve with the garnishing of fresh strawberries.

Nutrition Values Per Serving: Calories: 250; Fat: 13.6g; Sat Fat: 8.2g; Carbs: 30.7g; Fiber: 0.4g; Sugar: 22.1g; Protein: 2.4g

Blueberry Cobbler

Ingredients for Serving: 6

For the Filling:

2½ cups fresh blueberries.

1 tsp. fresh lemon juice

1 cup sugar

1 tsp. vanilla extract.

1 tbsp. butter, melted.

1 tsp. flour

For Topping:

1¾ cups all-purpose flour.

6 tbsp. sugar

1 cup milk

4 tsp. baking powder

5 tbsp. butter.

For Sprinkling:

¼ tsp. ground cinnamon.

2 tsp. sugar

Directions and Ready in About: 35-Minutes.

For filling:

- in a bowl, add all the filling ingredients and mix until well combined.

For topping:

- In another large bowl, mix together the flour, baking powder and sugar.
- Add the milk and butter and mix until a crumply mixture forms.

For sprinkling:

- In a small bowl mix together the sugar and cinnamon.
- In the bottom of a greased pan, place the blueberries mixture and top with the flour mixture evenly. Sprinkle the cinnamon sugar on top evenly.
- Press *Power* button of "Ninja Foodi Digital Air Fry Oven" and turn the dial to select *Air Fry* mode. Press *Time/Slice* button and again turn the dial to set the cooking time to 20 minutes.
- Now, push *Temp/Darkness* button and rotate the dial to set the temperature at 320 Degrees °F or (160 Degrees °C).
- Press *Start/Pause* button to start your Air Fry Oven. When the unit beeps to show that it is preheated, open the oven door.
- Arrange the pan in air fry basket and insert in the oven. When cooking time is complete, open the oven door and

place the pan onto a wire rack to cool for about 10 minutes before serving. Serve with the topping of vanilla ice cream.

Nutrition Values Per Serving: Calories: 459; Fat: 12.6g; Sat Fat: 7.8g; Carbs: 84g; Fiber: 2.7g; Sugar: 53.6g; Protein: 5.5g

Short-bread Fingers

Ingredients for Serving: 10

1⅔ cups plain flour.   ¾ cup butte

⅓ cup caster sugar

Directions and Ready in About: 27-Minutes.

- Take a large bowl, mix together the sugar and flour. Add the butter and mix until a smooth dough forms. Cut the dough into 10 equal-sized fingers. With a fork, lightly prick the fingers.
- Place the fingers into the lightly greased sheet pan. Press *Power* button of "Ninja Foodi Digital Air Fry Oven" and turn the dial to select *Air Fry* mode. Press *Time/Slice* button and again turn the dial to set the cooking time to 12 minutes.
- Now, push *Temp/Darkness* button and rotate the dial to set the temperature at 355 Degrees °F or (179 Degrees °C). Press *Start/Pause* button to start your Air Fry Oven. When the unit beeps to show that it is preheated, open the oven door.
- Arrange the pan in air fry basket and insert in the oven. When cooking time is completed, open the oven door and place the baking pan onto a wire rack to cool for about 5-10 minutes.
- Now, invert the shortbread fingers onto the wire rack to completely cool before serving. Serve with a dusting of powdered sugar.

Nutrition Values Per Serving: Calories: 223; Fat: 14g; Sat Fat: 8.8g; Carbs: 22.6g; Fiber: 0.6g; Sugar: 0.7g; Protein: 2.3g

Fried Doughnuts

Ingredients for Serving: 8

¼ cup/1 tsp. granulated sugar.

2 cups all-purpose flour

½ cup milk

4 tbsp. melted butter.

1 large egg

2 ¼ tsp. active dry yeast

½ tsp. kosher salt

1 tsp. pure vanilla extract.

Cooking spray

Directions and Ready in About: 21-Minutes.

- Warm up the milk in a suitable saucepan, then add yeast and 1 tsp. of sugar. Mix well and leave this milk for 8 minutes. Add flour, salt, butter, egg, vanilla and ¼ cup of sugar to the warm milk.
- Mix well and knead over a floured surface until smooth. Place this dough in a lightly greased bowl and brush it with cooking oil. Cover the prepared dough and leave it in a warm place for 1 hour.
- Punch the raised dough, then roll into ½ inch thick rectangle. Cut 3" circles out of this dough sheet using a biscuit cutter. Now, cut the rounds from the center to make a hole.

- Place the doughnuts in the air fry basket. Transfer the basket to the "Ninja Foodi Digital Air Fry Oven" and close the door.
- Select *Air Fry* mode by rotating the dial. Press the *Time/Slice* button and change the value to 6 minutes. Press the *Temp/Darkness* button and change the value to 375 Degrees °F or (190 Degrees °C).
- Press *Start/Pause* to begin cooking. Cook the doughnuts in batches to avoid overcrowding. Serve fresh with strawberry jam.

Nutrition Values Per Serving: Calories: 128; Fat: 20g; Carbs: 27g; Fiber: 0.9g; Sugar: 19g; Protein: 5.2g-

Caramel Apple Pie

Ingredients for Serving: 6

For the Topping:

⅓ cup packed brown sugar.

¼ cup all-purpose flour

2 tbsp. butter, softened.

½ tsp. ground cinnamon

For the Pie:

1 can (5 ounces) evaporated milk.

1 unbaked pastry shell (9 inches)

28 caramels

½ cup sugar

6 cups sliced peeled tart apples.

3 tbsp. all-purpose flour

1 tbsp. lemon juice.

½ tsp. ground cinnamon

Directions and Ready in About: 1 hr. 3-Minutes.

- Mix flour with cinnamon, butter and brown sugar. Spread this mixture in an 8-inch baking pan. Transfer the pan to the "Ninja Foodi Digital Air Fry Oven" and close the door.
- Select *Bake* mode by rotating the dial. Press the *Time/Slice* button and change the value to 8 minutes. Press the *Temp/Darkness* button and change the value to 350 Degrees °F or (176 Degrees °C). Press *Start/Pause* to begin cooking.
- Meanwhile, mix apple with lemon juice, cinnamon, flour and sugar. Spread the filling in the baked crust and return to the air fryer oven.
- Bake again for 35 minutes in the oven. Mix caramels with milk in a pan and cook until melted. Spread the caramel on top of the pie and bake for 5 minutes. Serve with apple sauce on top.

Nutrition Values Per Serving: Calories: 203; Fat: 8.9g; Carbs: 24.7g; Fiber: 1.2g; Sugar: 11.3g; Protein: 5.3g

Brownie Muffins

Ingredients for Serving: 12

1 package Betty Crocker fudge brownie mix.

⅓ cup vegetable oil

¼ cup walnuts, chopped.

1 egg

2 tsp. water.

Directions and Ready in About: 20-Minutes.

- Grease 12 muffin molds. Set aside. Take a bowl, mix together all the ingredients. Place the mixture into the prepared muffin molds.
- Press *Power* button of "Ninja Foodi Digital Air Fry Oven" and turn the dial to select *Air Fry* mode. Press *Time/Slice* button and again turn the dial to set the cooking time to 10 minutes.
- Now, push *Temp/Darkness* button and rotate the dial to set the temperature at 300 Degrees °F or (149 Degrees °C). Press *Start/Pause* button to start your Air Fry Oven. When the unit beeps to show that it is preheated, open the oven door.
- Arrange the muffin molds into the air fry basket and insert in the oven. When cooking time is completed, open the oven door and place the muffin molds onto a wire rack to cool for about 10 minutes. Carefully invert the muffins onto the wire rack to completely cool before serving with the topping of coconut.

Nutrition Values Per Serving: Calories: 168; Fat: 8.9g; Sat Fat: 1.4g; Carbs: 20.8g; Fiber: 1.1g; Sugar: 14g; Protein: 2g

Butter Cake

Ingredients for Serving: 6

½ cup caster sugar

1⅓ cups plain flour, sifted.

½ cup milk

1 egg

3 oz. butter, softened.

1 tbsp. icing sugar.

Pinch of salt

Directions and Ready in About: 30-Minutes.

- Take a bowl, add the butter and sugar and whisk until light and creamy. Add the egg and whisk until smooth and fluffy. Add the flour and salt and mix well alternately with the milk. Grease a small Bundt cake pan.
- Place mixture evenly into the prepared cake pan. Press *Power* button of "Ninja Foodi Digital Air Fry Oven" and turn the dial to select *Air Fry* mode. Press *Time/Slice* button and again turn the dial to set the cooking time to 15 minutes.
- Now, push *Temp/Darkness* button and rotate the dial to set the temperature at 350 Degrees °F or (176 Degrees °C). Press *Start/Pause* button to start your Air Fry Oven. When the unit beeps to show that it is preheated, open the oven door.
- Arrange the pan into the air fry basket and insert in the oven. When cooking time is completed, open the oven door and place the cake pan onto a wire rack to cool for about 10 minutes.
- Carefully invert the cake onto the wire rack to completely cool before slicing. Dust the cake with icing sugar and cut into desired size slices. Serve with the sprinkling of cocoa powder.

Nutrition Values Per Serving: Calories: 291; Fat: 12.9g; Sat Fat: 7.8g; Carbs: 40.3g; Fiber: 0.8g; Sugar: 19g; Protein: 4.6g

Chocolate Soufflé

Ingredients for Serving: 2

3 oz. semi-sweet chocolate, chopped.

2 eggs, yolks and whites separated

2 tbsp. all-purpose flour

¼ cup butter.

3 tbsp. sugar

½ tsp. pure vanilla extract.

1 tsp. powdered sugar plus extra for dusting

Directions and Ready in About: 31-Minutes.

- In a microwave-safe bowl, place the butter and chocolate. Microwave on high heat for about 2 minutes or until melted completely, stirring after every 30 seconds. Remove from the microwave and stir the mixture until smooth.
- In another bowl, add the egg yolks and whisk well. Add the sugar and vanilla extract and whisk well. Add the chocolate mixture and mix until well combined. Add the flour and mix well.
- In a clean glass bowl, add the egg whites and whisk until soft peaks form. Fold the whipped egg whites in 3 portions into the chocolate mixture.
- Grease 2 ramekins and sprinkle each with a pinch of sugar. Place mixture into the prepared ramekins and with the back of a spoon, smooth the top surface.
- Press *Power* button of "Ninja Foodi Digital Air Fry Oven" and turn the dial to select *Air Fry* mode. Press *Time/Slice* button and again turn the dial to set the cooking time to 14 minutes.
- Now, push *Temp/Darkness* button and rotate the dial to set the temperature at 330 Degrees °F or (166 Degrees °C). Press *Start/Pause* button to start your Air Fry Oven.
- When the unit beeps to show that it is preheated, open the oven door. Arrange the ramekins into the air fry basket and insert in the oven.
- When cooking time is completed, open the oven door and place the ramekins onto a wire rack to cool slightly. Sprinkle with the powdered sugar and serve warm with the garnishing of berries.

Nutrition Values Per Serving: Calories: 591; Fat: 87.3g; Sat Fat: 23g; Carbs: 52.6g; Fiber: 0.2g; Sugar: 41.1g; Protein: 9.4g

Fudge Brownies

Ingredients for Serving: 8

½ cup butter, melted.

⅓ cup cocoa powder

1 cup sugar.

½ cup flour

2 eggs

1 tsp. baking powder.

1 tsp. vanilla extract

Directions and Ready in About: 35-Minutes.

- Grease a baking pan. Take a large bowl, add the sugar and butter and whisk until light and fluffy. Add the remaining ingredients and mix until well combined. Place mixture into the prepared pan and with the back of a spatula, smooth the top surface.

- Press *Power* button of "Ninja Foodi Digital Air Fry Oven" and turn the dial to select *Air Fry* mode. Press *Time/Slice* button and again turn the dial to set the cooking time to 20 minutes.
- Now, push *Temp/Darkness* button and rotate the dial to set the temperature at 350 Degrees °F or (176 Degrees °C). Press *Start/Pause* button to start your Air Fry Oven. When the unit beeps to show that it is preheated, open the oven door.
- Arrange the pan in air fry basket and insert in the oven. When cooking time is completed, open the oven door and place the sheet pan onto a wire rack to cool completely. Cut into 8 equal-sized squares and serve with a drizzling of melted chocolate.

Nutrition Values Per Serving: Calories: 250; Fat: 13.2g; Sat Fat: 7.9g; Carbs: 33.4g; Fiber: 1.3g; Sugar: 25.2g; Protein: 3g

Cherry Clafoutis

Ingredients for Serving: 4

1½ cups fresh cherries, pitted.	1 egg
¼ cup powdered sugar	2 tbsp. sugar.
½ cup sour cream.	3 tbsp. vodka
¼ cup flour	1 tbsp. butter
	Pinch of salt.

Directions and Ready in About: 40-Minutes.

- Take a bowl, mix together the cherries and vodka. In another bowl, mix together the flour, sugar and salt. Add the sour cream and egg and mix until a smooth dough forms.
- Grease a cake pan. Place flour mixture evenly into the prepared cake pan. Spread cherry mixture over the dough. Place butter on top in the form of dots.
- Press *Power* button of "Ninja Foodi Digital Air Fry Oven" and turn the dial to select *Air Fry* mode. Press *Time/Slice* button and again turn the dial to set the cooking time to 25 minutes.
- Now, push *Temp/Darkness* button and rotate the dial to set the temperature at 355 Degrees °F or (179 Degrees °C). Press *Start/Pause* button to start your Air Fry Oven. When the unit beeps to show that it is preheated, open the oven door.
- Arrange the pan in air fry basket and insert in the oven. When cooking time is completed, open the oven door and place the pan onto a wire rack to cool for about 10-15 minutes before serving.
- Now, invert the Clafoutis onto a platter and sprinkle with powdered sugar. Cut the Clafoutis into desired sized slices and serve warm with a topping of whipped cream.

Nutrition Values Per Serving: Calories: 241; Fat: 10.1g; Sat Fat: 5.9g; Carbs: 29g; Fiber: 1.3g; Sugar: 20.6g; Protein: 3.9g

Apple Pastries

Ingredients for Serving: 6

7.5 oz. prepared frozen puff pastry.	1 tsp. fresh orange zest, grated finely
½ of large apple, peeled, cored and chopped	½ tsp. ground cinnamon.
	½ tbsp. white sugar.

Directions and Ready in About: 25-Minutes.

- Take a bowl, mix together all ingredients except puff pastry. Cut the pastry in 16 squares. Place about a tsp. of the apple mixture in the center of each square. Fold each square into a triangle and press the edges slightly with wet fingers.
- Then with a fork, press the edges firmly. Press *Power* button of "Ninja Foodi Digital Air Fry Oven" and turn the dial to select *Air Fry* mode. Press *Time/Slice* button and again turn the dial to set the cooking time to 10 minutes.
- Now, push *Temp/Darkness* button and rotate the dial to set the temperature at 390 Degrees °F or (199 Degrees °C). Press *Start/Pause* button to start your Air Fry Oven. When the unit beeps to show that it is preheated, open the oven door.
- Arrange the pastries in the greased air fry basket and insert in the oven. When cooking time is completed, open the oven door and transfer the pastries onto a platter. Serve warm with a dusting of powdered sugar.

Nutrition Values Per Serving: Calories: 198; Fat: 12.7g; Sat Fat: 3.2g; Carbs: 18.8g; Fiber: 1.1g; Sugar: 3.2g; Protein: 2.5g

Vanilla Bread Pudding

Ingredients for Serving: 3

2 bread slices, cut into small cubes.	1 egg
2 tbsp. raisins, soaked in hot water for 15 minutes.	1 tbsp. brown sugar
1 cup milk	1 tbsp. sugar
	½ tsp. ground cinnamon.
	¼ tsp. vanilla extract

Directions and Ready in About: 27-Minutes.

- Take a bowl, mix together the milk, egg, brown sugar, cinnamon and vanilla extract. Stir in the raisins. In a baking pan, spread the bread cubes and top evenly with the milk mixture. Refrigerate for about 15-20 minutes.
- Press *Power* button of "Ninja Foodi Digital Air Fry Oven" and turn the dial to select *Air Fry* mode. Press *Time/Slice* button and again turn the dial to set the cooking time to 12 minutes.
- Now, push *Temp/Darkness* button and rotate the dial to set the temperature at 375 Degrees °F or (190 Degrees °C). Press *Start/Pause* button to start your Air Fry Oven. When the unit beeps to show that it is preheated, open the oven door.
- Arrange the pan over the wire rack and insert in the oven. When cooking time is completed, open the oven door and place the baking pan aside to cool slightly. Serve warm with the drizzling of vanilla syrup.

Nutrition Values Per Serving: Calories: 143; Fat: 4.4g; Sat Fat: 2.2g; Carbs: 21.3g; Fiber: 6.7g; Sugar: 16.4g; Protein: 5.5g

Nutella Banana Muffins

Ingredients for Serving: 12

4 ripe bananas, peeled and mashed.

2 eggs

¼ cup walnuts

1⅔ cups plain flour.

½ cup brown sugar

3 tbsp. milk.

1 tbsp. Nutella

1 tsp. baking soda.

1 tsp. baking powder

1 tsp. ground cinnamon.

¼ tsp. salt

1 tsp. vanilla essence

Directions and Ready in About: 40-Minutes.

- Grease 12 muffin molds. Set aside. Take a large bowl, put together the flour, baking soda, baking powder, cinnamon and salt. In another bowl, mix together the remaining ingredients except walnuts. Add the banana mixture into flour mixture and mix until just combined. Fold in the walnuts.
- Place the mixture into the prepared muffin molds. Press *Power* button of "Ninja Foodi Digital Air Fry Oven" and turn the dial to select *Air Fry* mode. Press *Time/Slice* button and again turn the dial to set the cooking time to 25 minutes.
- Now, push *Temp/Darkness* button and rotate the dial to set the temperature at 250 Degrees °F or (121 Degrees °C). Press *Start/Pause* button to start your Air Fry Oven. When the unit beeps to show that it is preheated, open the oven door.
- Arrange the muffin molds in air fry basket and insert in the oven. When cooking time is completed, open the oven door and place the muffin molds onto a wire rack to cool for about 10 minutes. Carefully, invert the muffins onto the wire rack to completely cool before serving serve with a glass of milk.

Nutrition Values Per Serving: Calories: 227; Fat: 6.6g; Sat Fat: 1.5g; Carbs: 38.1g; Fiber: 2.4g; Sugar: 15.8g; Protein: 5.2g

Cinnamon Banana

Ingredients for Serving: 2

1 ripe banana, peeled and sliced lengthwise.

⅛ tsp. ground cinnamon

½ tsp. fresh lemon juice.

2 tsp. honey

Directions and Ready in About: 20-Minutes.

- Coat each banana half with lemon juice. Arrange the banana halves onto the greased sheet pan cut sides up. Drizzle the banana halves with honey and sprinkle with cinnamon.
- Press *Power* button of "Ninja Foodi Digital Air Fry Oven" and turn the dial to select *Air Fry* mode. Press *Time/Slice* button and again turn the dial to set the cooking time to 10 minutes.
- Now, push *Temp/Darkness* button and rotate the dial to set the temperature at 350 Degrees °F or (176 Degrees °C). Press *Start/Pause* button to start your Air Fry

Oven. When the unit beeps to show that it is preheated, open the oven door.

- Insert the sheet pan in oven. When cooking time is completed, open the oven door and transfer the banana slices onto a platter. Serve immediately with garnishing of almonds.

Nutrition Values Per Serving: Calories: 74; Fat: 0.2g; Sat Fat: 0.1g; Carbs: 19.4g; Fiber: 1.6g; Sugar: 13g; Protein: 0.7g

Brownie Bars

Ingredients for Serving: 8

For Brownie:

1 oz. unsweetened chocolate.

1 cup walnuts, chopped.

2 large eggs, beaten.

½ cup butter, cubed.

1 tsp. vanilla extract.

1 cup sugar

1 cup all-purpose flour

1 tsp. baking powder.

For the Filling:

¼ cup butter, softened

6 oz. cream cheese softened

1 large egg, beaten

2 tbsp. all-purpose flour

½ cup sugar

½ tsp. vanilla extract

For the Topping:

2 cups mini marshmallows

1 cup (6 ounces) chocolate chips

1 cup walnuts, chopped.

For the Topping:

2 oz. cream cheese.

1 oz. unsweetened chocolate

¼ cup butter

3 cups confectioners' sugar.

¼ cup milk

1 tsp. vanilla extract.

Directions and Ready in About: 43-Minutes.

- Take a small bowl, add and whisk all the ingredients for filling until smooth. Melt butter with chocolate in a large saucepan over medium heat. Mix well, then remove the melted chocolate from the heat.
- Now, stir in vanilla, eggs, baking powder, flour, sugar and nuts then mix well. Spread this chocolate batter in the sheet pan. Drizzle nuts, marshmallows and chocolate chips over the batter. Transfer the pan to the "Ninja Foodi Digital Air Fry Oven" and close the door.
- Select *Air Fry* mode by rotating the dial. Press the *Time/Slice* button and change the value to 28 minutes. Press the *Temp/Darkness* button and change the value to 350 Degrees °F or (176 Degrees °C). Press *Start/Pause* to begin cooking.
- Meanwhile, prepare the frosting by heating butter with cream cheese, chocolate and milk in a suitable saucepan over medium heat. Mix well, then remove it from the heat.
- Stir in vanilla and sugar, then mix well. Pour this frosting over the brownie. Allow the brownie to cool then slice

into bars. Serve with whipped cream and chocolate syrup on top.

Nutrition Values Per Serving: Calories: 298; Fat: 14g; Sodium: 272mg; Carbs: 34g; Fiber: 1g; Sugar: 9.3g; Protein: 13g

Blueberry Hand Pies

Ingredients for Serving: 6

14 oz. refrigerated pie crust.	1 pinch salt
1 cup blueberries	vanilla sugar to sprinkle on top.
2 ½ tbsp. caster sugar.	water
1 tsp. lemon juice	

Directions and Ready in About: 40-Minutes.

- Toss the blueberries with salt, lemon juice and sugar in a medium bowl. Spread the pie crust into a round sheet and cut 6-by-4-inch circles out of it.
- Add a tbsp. of blueberry filling at the center of each circle. Moisten the edges of these circles and fold them in half, then pinch their edges together.
- Press the edges using a fork to crimp its edges. Place the hand pies in the air fry basket and spray them with cooking oil. Drizzle the vanilla sugar over the hand pies. Transfer the blueberry hand pies to the "Ninja Foodi Digital Air Fry Oven" and close the door.
- Select *Air Fry* mode by rotating the dial. Press the *Time/Slice* button and change the value to 25 minutes. Press the *Temp/Darkness* button and change the value to 400 Degrees °F or (204 Degrees °C). Press *Start/Pause* to begin cooking. Serve fresh with cream frosting and blueberry sauce on top.

Nutrition Values Per Serving: Calories: 253; Fat: 14g; Sodium: 122mg; Carbs: 36g; Fiber: 1.2g; Sugar: 12g; Protein: 12g

Peanut Brittle Bars

Ingredients for Serving: 6

1 cup packed brown sugar.	½ cup whole wheat flour
1-½ cups all-purpose flour	1 tsp. baking soda
1 cup butter.	¼ tsp. salt.

For the Topping:

12 ¼ oz. caramel ice cream topping.	1 cup milk chocolate chips.
2 cups salted peanuts	3 tbsp. all-purpose flour

Directions and Ready in About: 43-Minutes.

- Mix flours with salt, baking soda and brown sugar in a large bowl. Spread the batter in a greased sheet pan. Transfer the pan to the "Ninja Foodi Digital Air Fry Oven" and close the door.
- Select *Bake* mode by rotating the dial. Press the *Time/Slice* button and change the value to 12 minutes. Press the *Temp/Darkness* button and change the value to 350 Degrees °F or (176 Degrees °C). Press *Start/Pause* to begin cooking.

- Spread chocolate chips and peanuts on top. Mix flour with caramels topping in a bowl and spread on top, Bake again for 16 minutes. Serve with sweet cream cheese dip.

Nutrition Values Per Serving: Calories: 153; Fat: 1g; Sodium: 8mg; Carbs: 26g; Fiber: 0.8g; Sugar: 56g; Protein: 11g

Cherry Jam tarts

Ingredients for Serving: 6

2 sheets shortcrust pastry.

For the frangipane:

4 oz. ground almonds.	4 oz. butter softened.
3 oz. cherry jam	1 egg
4 oz. golden caster sugar	1 tbsp. plain flour

For the icing:

12 glacé cherries.	1 cup icing sugar

Directions and Ready in About: 55-Minutes.

- Grease the 12 cups of the muffin tray with butter. Roll the puff pastry into a 10 cm sheet, then cut 12 rounds out of it. Place these rounds into each muffin cup and press them into these cups. Transfer the muffin tray to the refrigerator and leave it for 20 minutes.
- Add dried beans or pulses into each tart crust to add weight. Transfer the muffin tray to the "Ninja Foodi Digital Air Fry Oven" and close the door.
- Select *Bake* mode by rotating the dial. Press the *Time/Slice* button and change the value to 10 minutes. Press the *Temp/Darkness* button and change the value to 350 Degrees °F or (176 Degrees °C).
- Press *Start/Pause* to begin cooking. Now, remove the dried beans from the crust and bake again for 10 minutes in the Ninja Foodi Digital Air Fry oven.
- Meanwhile, prepare the filling beat, beat butter with sugar and egg until fluffy. Stir in flour and almonds ground, then mix well.
- Divide this filling in the baked crusts and top them with a tbsp. of cherry jam. Now, again, place the muffin tray in the Ninja Foodi Digital Air Fry oven.
- Continue cooking on the *Bake* mode for 20 minutes at 350 Degrees °F or (176 Degrees °C). Whisk the icing sugar with 2 tbsp. water and top the baked tarts with sugar mixture. Serve with cherries on top.

Nutrition Values Per Serving: Calories: 193; Fat: 3g; Sodium: 277mg; Carbs: 21g; Fiber: 1g; Sugar: 9g; Protein: 2g

Blueberry Muffins

Ingredients for Serving: 6

1 ripe banana, peeled and mashed.	1 tbsp. coconut oil, melted
⅛ cup maple syrup	½ tsp. baking powder.
1¼ cups almond flour.	1 tsp. apple cider vinegar
½ cup fresh blueberries	1 tsp. vanilla extract
1 egg, beaten	1 tsp. lemon zest, grated.
2 tbsp. granulated sugar.	Pinch of ground cinnamon

Directions and Ready in About: 27-Minutes.

- Take a large bowl, add all the ingredients except for blueberries and mix until well combined. Gently fold in the blueberries. Grease a 6-cup muffin pan.
- Place the mixture into prepared muffin cups about ¾ full. Press *Power* button of "Ninja Foodi Digital Air Fry Oven" and turn the dial to select *Bake* mode. Press *Time/Slice* button and again turn the dial to set the cooking time to 12 minutes.
- Now, push *Temp/Darkness* button and rotate the dial to set the temperature at 375 Degrees °F or (190 Degrees °C). Press *Start/Pause* button to start your Air Fry Oven.
- When the unit beeps to show that it is preheated, open the oven door. Arrange the muffin pan over the wire rack and insert in the oven.
- When cooking time is completed, open the oven door and place the muffin molds onto a wire rack to cool for about 10 minutes. Carefully invert the muffins onto the wire rack to completely cool before serving. Serve with a hot cup of coffee.

Nutrition Values Per Serving: Calories: 223; Fat: 14.8g; Sat Fat: 3g; Carbs: 20.1g; Fiber: 3.4g; Sugar: 12.5g; Protein: 6.2g

Cranberry Apple Pie

Ingredients for Serving: 8

½ cup cold unsalted butter, cubed.	7 tbsp. ice water
⅓ cup cold shortening	1 tbsp. sugar
2 ½ cups all-purpose flour.	¾ tsp. salt

For the Filling:

6 baking apples, peeled and cut into slices	2 tbsp. dark rum
1 cup fresh cranberries, divided.	2 tbsp. tapioca
¾ cup sugar, divided.	1 tbsp. lemon juice.
½ cup dried currants or raisins.	2 tsp. grated lemon zest
	½ tsp. ground cinnamon

Egg Wash

1 large egg	2 tsp. sugar
1 tbsp. milk.	Dash ground cinnamon.

Directions and Ready in About: 1 hr.

- Mix flour with butter, salt and sugar in a bowl. Stir in water and mix well until smooth. Divide the prepared dough into two halves and spread each into a ⅛-inch-thick round.
- Blend cranberries with sugar in a food processor. Transfer to a bowl and stir in remaining filling ingredients. Spread one dough round on a 9-inch pie plate. Spread the prepared filling in the crust.
- Slice the other dough round into strips and make a crisscross pattern on top. Brush the pie with egg and milk mixture, then drizzle sugar and cinnamon top.
- Transfer the pan to the "Ninja Foodi Digital Air Fry Oven" and close the door. Select *Bake* mode by rotating the

dial. Press the *Time/Slice* button and change the value to 45 minutes. Press the *Temp/Darkness* button and change the value to 325 Degrees °F or (163 Degrees °C).
- Press *Start/Pause* to begin cooking. Cool on a wire rack for 30 minutes. Serve with whipped cream on top.

Nutrition Values Per Serving: Calories: 145; Fat: 3g; Sodium: 355mg; Carbs: 20g; Fiber: 1g; Sugar: 25g; Protein: 1g

Chocolate Bites

Ingredients for Serving: 8

¼ cup chocolate, chopped. into 8 chunks.	½ cup icing sugar
¾ cup chilled butter	2 tbsp. cocoa powder
2 cups plain flour.	Pinch of ground cinnamon.
	1 tsp. vanilla extract

Directions and Ready in About: 28-Minutes.

- Take a bowl, mix together the flour, icing sugar, cocoa powder, cinnamon and vanilla extract. With a pastry cutter, cut the butter and mix till a smooth dough forms. Divide the dough into 8 equal-sized balls.
- Press 1 chocolate chunk in the center of each ball and cover with the dough completely. Place the balls into the sheet pan. Press *Power* button of Ninja Foodi Air Fry Digital Oven and turn the dial to select the *Air Fry* mode. Press *Time/Slice* button and again turn the dial to set the cooking time to 8 minutes.
- Now, push *Temp/Darkness* button and rotate the dial to set the temperature at 355 Degrees °F or (179 Degrees °C). Press *Start/Pause* button to start your Air Fry Oven.
- When the unit beeps to show that it is preheated, open the oven door. Arrange the pan in air fry basket and insert in the oven. After 8 minutes of cooking, set the temperature at 320 Degrees °F or (160 Degrees °C) for 5 minutes.
- When cooking time is completed, open the oven door and place the sheet pan onto the wire rack to cool completely before serving. Serve with a sprinkling of coconut shreds.

Nutrition Values Per Serving: Calories: 328; Fat: 19.3g; Sat Fat: 12.2g; Carbs: 35.3g; Fiber: 1.4g; Sugar: 10.2g; Protein: 4.1g

Carrot Mug Cake

Ingredients for Serving: 1

¼ cup whole-wheat pastry flour.	¼ tsp. baking powder
2 tbsp. plus 2 tsp. unsweetened almond milk	⅛ tsp. ground cinnamon
2 tbsp. carrot, peeled and grated.	2 tsp. applesauce.
2 tbsp. walnuts, chopped.	⅛ tsp. ground ginger
1 tbsp. raisins	Pinch of salt
1 tbsp. coconut sugar.	Pinch of ground cloves.
	Pinch of ground allspice

Directions and Ready in About: 30-Minutes.

- Take a bowl, mix together the flour, sugar, baking powder, spices and salt. Add the remaining ingredients and mix until well combined. Place the mixture into a lightly greased ramekin.
- Press *Power* button of "Ninja Foodi Digital Air Fry Oven" and turn the dial to select the *Bake* mode. Press *Time/Slice* button and again turn the dial to set the cooking time to 20 minutes.
- Now, push *Temp/Darkness* button and rotate the dial to set the temperature at 350 Degrees °F or (176 Degrees °C). Press *Start/Pause* button to start your Air Fry Oven. When the unit beeps to show that it is preheated, open the oven door.
- Arrange the ramekin over the wire rack and insert in the oven. When cooking time is completed, open the oven door and place the ramekin onto a wire rack to cool slightly before serving. Serve with the topping of whipped cream.

Nutrition Values Per Serving: Calories: 301; Fat: 10.1g; Sat Fat: 0.7g; Carbs: 48.6g; Fiber: 3.2g; Sugar: 19.4g; Protein: 7.6g

Mouth Watering Cannoli

Ingredients for Serving: 4

For the Filling:

1 (16-ounce) container ricotta.	¾ cup heavy cream
½ cup mini chocolate chips, for garnish	½ cup mascarpone cheese.
½ cup powdered sugar, divided.	1 tsp. orange zest
	1 tsp. vanilla extract
	¼ tsp. kosher salt.

For Shells:

¼ cup granulated sugar.	1 large egg
1 egg white for brushing	6 tbsp. white wine
2 cups all-purpose flour.	1 tsp. kosher salt
4 tbsp. cold butter, cut into cubes.	½ tsp. cinnamon.
	Vegetable oil for frying

Directions and Ready in About: 27-Minutes.

- For the filling, beat all the ingredients in a mixer and fold in whipped cream. Cover and refrigerate this filling for 1 hour. Mix all the shell ingredients in a bowl until smooth.
- Cover this dough and refrigerate for 1 hour. Roll the prepared dough into a ⅛-inch-thick sheet. Cut 4 small circles out of the prepared dough and wrap it around the cannoli molds.
- Brush the prepared dough with egg whites to seal the edges. Place the shells in the air fry basket. Transfer the basket to the "Ninja Foodi Digital Air Fry Oven" and close the door.
- Select *Air Fry* mode by rotating the dial. Press the *Time/Slice* button and change the value to 12 minutes. Press the *Temp/Darkness* button and change the value to 350 Degrees °F or (176 Degrees °C). Press *Start/Pause* to begin cooking.

- Place filling in a pastry bag fitted with an open star tip. Pipe filling into shells, then dip ends in mini chocolate chips. Transfer the prepared filling to a piping bag. Pipe the filling into the cannoli shells. Serve with chocolate chips and chocolate syrup.

Nutrition Values Per Serving: Calories: 348; Fat: 16g; Sodium: 95mg; Carbs: 38.4g; Fiber: 0.3g; Sugar: 10g; Protein: 14g

Nutella Banana Pastries

Ingredients for Serving: 4

2 bananas, peeled and sliced.	1 puff pastry sheet
	½ cup Nutella.

Directions and Ready in About: 27-Minutes.

- Cut the pastry sheet into 4 equal-sized squares. Spread the Nutella on each square of pastry evenly. Divide the banana slices over Nutella. Fold each square into a triangle and with wet fingers, slightly press the edges. Then with a fork, press the edges firmly.
- Press *Power* button of "Ninja Foodi Digital Air Fry Oven" and turn the dial to select *Air Fry* mode. Press *Time/Slice* button and again turn the dial to set the cooking time to 12 minutes.
- Now, push *Temp/Darkness* button and rotate the dial to set the temperature at 375 Degrees °F or (190 Degrees °C). Press *Start/Pause* button to start your Air Fry Oven.
- When the unit beeps to show that it is preheated, open the oven door. Arrange the pastries into the greased air fry basket and insert in the oven. When cooking time is completed, open the oven door and serve warm with the sprinkling of cinnamon.

Nutrition Values Per Serving: Calories: 221; Fat: 10g; Sat Fat: 2.7g; Carbs: 31.6g; Fiber: 2.6g; Sugar: 14.4g; Protein: 3.4g

Fried Churros

Ingredients for Serving: 8

1 cup all-purpose flour.	2 tbsp. granulated sugar
2 large eggs	¼ tsp. salt
1 cup water	1 tsp. vanilla extract.
⅓ cup butter, cut into cubes.	oil spray

Cinnamon Coating:

¾ tsp. ground cinnamon.	½ cup granulated sugar

Directions and Ready in About: 27-Minutes.

- Grease the sheet pan with cooking spray. Warm water with butter, salt and sugar in a suitable saucepan until it boils. Now, reduce its heat, then slowly stir in flour and mix well until smooth.
- Remove the mixture from the heat and leave it for 4 minutes to cool. Add vanilla extract and eggs, then beat the mixture until it comes together as a batter.
- Transfer this churro mixture to a piping bag with star-shaped tips and pipe the batter on the prepared pan to get 4-inch churros using this batter.

- Refrigerate these churros for 1 hour, then transfer them to the Air fry sheet. Transfer the sheet to the "Ninja Foodi Digital Air Fry Oven" and close the door.
- Select *Air Fry* mode by rotating the dial. Press the *Temp/Darkness* button and change the value to 375 Degrees °F or (190 Degrees °C). Press the *Time/Slice* button and change the value to 12 minutes, then press *Start/Pause* to begin cooking.
- Meanwhile, mix granulated sugar with cinnamon in a bowl. Drizzle this mixture over the air fried churros. Serve with chocolate dip.

Nutrition Values Per Serving: Calories: 278; Fat: 10g; Sodium: 218mg; Carbs: 26g; Fiber: 10g; Sugar: 30g; Protein: 4g

Vanilla Soufflé

Ingredients for Serving: 6

½ cup plus 2 tbsp. sugar, divided.	1 cup milk
¼ cup butter, softened	3 tsp. vanilla extract, divided.
¼ cup all-purpose flour.	2 tbsp. powdered sugar plus extra for dusting.
5 egg whites	
4 egg yolks.	1 tsp. cream of tartar

Directions and Ready in About: 38-Minutes.

- Take a bowl, add the butter and flour and mix until a smooth paste forms. In a medium pan, mix together ½ cup of sugar and milk over medium-low heat and cook for about 3 minutes or until the sugar is dissolved, stirring continuously.
- Add the flour mixture, whisking continuously and simmer for about 3-4 minutes or until mixture becomes thick. Remove from the heat and stir in 1 tsp. of vanilla extract. Set aside for about 10 minutes to cool.
- Take a bowl, add the egg yolks and 1 tsp. of vanilla extract and mix well. Add the egg yolk mixture into milk mixture and mix until well combined.
- In another bowl, add the egg whites, cream of tartar, remaining sugar and vanilla extract and with a wire whisk, beat until stiff peaks form.
- Fold the egg white mixture into milk mixture. Grease 6 ramekins and sprinkle each with a pinch of sugar.
- Place mixture into the prepared ramekins and with the back of a spoon, smooth the top surface. Press *Power* button of "Ninja Foodi Digital Air Fry Oven" and turn the dial to select *Air Fry* mode. Press *Time/Slice* button and again turn the dial to set the cooking time to 16 minutes.
- Now, push *Temp/Darkness* button and rotate the dial to set the temperature at 330 Degrees °F or (166 Degrees °C). Press *Start/Pause* button to start your Air Fry Oven. When the unit beeps to show that it is preheated, open the oven door.
- Arrange the ramekins in air fry basket and insert in the oven. When cooking time is completed, open the oven door and place the ramekins onto a wire rack to cool slightly. Sprinkle with the powdered sugar and serve warm with caramel sauce.

Nutrition Values Per Serving: Calories: 250; Fat: 11.6g; Sat Fat: 6.5g; Carbs: 29.8g; Fiber: 0.1g; Sugar: 25g; Protein: 6.8g

Walnut Brownies

Ingredients for Serving: 4

½ cup chocolate, roughly chopped.	5 tbsp. sugar
1 egg, beaten	5 tbsp. self-rising flour.
¼ cup walnuts, chopped.	1 tsp. vanilla extract
⅓ cup butter	Pinch of salt

Directions and Ready in About: 37-Minutes.

- In a microwave-safe bowl, add the chocolate and butter. Microwave on high heat for about 2 minutes, stirring after every 30 seconds.
- Remove from microwave and set aside to cool. In another bowl, add the sugar, egg, vanilla extract and salt and whisk until creamy and light.
- Add the chocolate mixture and whisk until well combined. Add the flour and walnuts and mix until well combined. Line a baking pan with a greased parchment paper. Place mixture into the prepared pan and with the back of spatula, smooth the top surface.
- Press *Power* button of "Ninja Foodi Digital Air Fry Oven" and turn the dial to select *Air Fry* mode. Press *Time/Slice* button and again turn the dial to set the cooking time to 20 minutes.
- Now, push *Temp/Darkness* button and rotate the dial to set the temperature at 355 Degrees °F or (179 Degrees °C). Press *Start/Pause* button to start your Air Fry Oven. When the unit beeps to show that it is preheated, open the oven door.
- Arrange the pan into the air fry basket and insert in the oven. When cooking time is completed, open the oven door and place the baking pan onto a wire rack to cool completely. Cut into 4 equal-sized squares and serve with the dusting of powdered sugar.

Nutrition Values Per Serving: Calories: 407; Fat: 27.4g; Sat Fat: 14.7g; Carbs: 35.9g; Fiber: 1.5g; Sugar: 26.2g; Protein: 6g

Manufactured by Amazon.ca
Acheson, AB

11455578R00046